# *The Social Security Swindle – How Anyone Can Drop Out*

# *The Social Security Swindle – How Anyone Can Drop Out*

by

IRWIN SCHIFF

Freedom Books
Hamden, Connecticut

This book is designed to provide the author's findings and opinions based on research and analysis of the subject matter covered. This information is not provided for purposes of rendering legal or other professional services, which can only be provided by knowledgeable professionals on a fee basis.

Further, there is always an element of risk in standing up for one's lawful rights in the face of an oppressive taxing authority backed by a biased judiciary.

Therefore, the author and publisher disclaim any responsibility for any liability or loss incurred as a consequence of the use and application, either directly or indirectly, of any advice or information presented herein.





Library of Congress Catalog Card No. 83-90489

ISBN-0-930374-05-3

84 85 86 87 10 9 8 7 6 5 4 3 2 1

*TO*

Former Supreme Court Justices Pierce Butler and James C. McReynolds and former United States Circuit Judges James M. Morton, Jr. and Scott Wilson. By declaring Social Security unconstitutional in 1937, they demonstrated that they were members of a vanishing breed — Federal judges who understand and enforce the United States Constitution.

*Books By Irwin A. Schiff*

How Anyone Can Stop Paying Income Taxes

The Kingdom of Moltz

The Biggest Con: How The Government is Fleecing You

# Contents


INTRODUCTION .......... 11

1. Socialism Arrives in America .......... 15
2. Surprise! Social Security — Just Another "Income Tax" .......... 23
3. How To Stop Employers From Withholding "Social Security" Taxes .......... 39
4. Employers and Self—Employeds — How They, Too, Can Drop Out .......... 47
5. The Supreme Court — Playing Games With The Law .......... 65
6. How Social Security Was Sold To The Public — Would They Buy It Today? .......... 99
7. An Analysis of Government Studies: Proof That Government Cannot Be Trusted .......... 109
8. Of Taxes And Trust Funds .......... 163
9. The System Encourages Rampant Abuse .......... 173
10. Why Dropping Out Of Social Security Is In The National Interest .......... 191

Appendix A: Chapter 4 — *The Biggest Con–How The Government Is Fleecing You* .......... 209

Appendix B: Pages 302-304, *The Biggest Con* .......... 233

Appendix C: Sample Lawsuit .......... 239

Appendix D: Private Sector "Experts" .......... 243

Legal Cases Cited .......... 251

Reading List .......... 253

# *Introduction*

In October, 1934, after serving approximately 10 years in jail, a little Italian immigrant named Charles Ponzi was deported to Italy after pulling off one of the greatest swindles America had ever witnessed.

In December, 1919, Ponzi convinced about a dozen people that he could make them a 50% profit in 45 days by trading in international postal coupons.

At the end of the first 45 days his first batch of "investors" lined up to claim their profits. Sure enough, Ponzi was as good as his word and paid his investors $375.00 for the $250.00 initially given him. As Ponzi expected, most of his investors handed the money right back to him so he could reinvest it for them and then they fanned out into the community, spreading the news that Ponzi could make everyone rich.

The news spread quickly. Within a month thousands of people, money in hand, lined up in front of Ponzi's School Street office. He even hired 3 women to serve franks and coffee to those who had to wait. By

April of 1920 he was taking in $250,000 a day, had 16 clerks just taking in money and nearly as many guarding it.

In less than 6 months Ponzi collected over $10 million and his name was known from coast to coast. He refurbished his office and gave his company the impressive title, "SECURITIES EXCHANGE COMPANY". He purchased a 20 acre estate near Boston and spent $500,000 redecorating it. He supposedly spent $100,000 just stocking the wine cellar! He purchased large tracts of land and large interests in banks and investment companies.

A chauffeur and footman, outfitted in plum colored livery, squired him around the city in a custom built limousine. Everywhere he went he was beseiged by well-wishers who cheered him and implored him to take their money.

Ponzi's scheme collapsed when a spiteful former friend notified Boston police that Ponzi had served 3 years in a Montreal jail for forgery. This was confirmed by the Montreal police on April 11, 1920 when they supplied Boston authorities with a mug shot of Ponzi.

What Ponzi had done, of course, was simple...he used the money given him by new "investors" to pay off older "investors". As long as more money came in than had to be paid out, the scheme worked (in all such scams money will keep coming in as long as enough people believe that they, too, will make what others are reported to have made). He was even able to skim off considerable amounts for himself to create and maintain a lavish personal and business life-style.

What promoters of such swindles hope to do, of course, is to vanish with enough loot before the last round of victims realize they have been taken. Early "winners" are necessary in order for the scam to work.

Such swindles, however, depend on an ever expanding army of new participants relative to those who drop out. When the tide turns, the scam inevitably collapses. The losses sustained by all those left holding the bag at the end finance the gains realized by earlier participants and the "profit" that the promoters skimmed off.

Chain letters and pyramid schemes are variations of the Ponzi scam and rely, more or less, on the same principle. Americans have now been victimized by the greatest Ponzi swindle of them all - SOCIAL SECURITY! It really isn't any different from the scheme devised by Ponzi some 60 years ago - it's only bigger. It would not be inappropriate for the Social Security Administration to commission a large statue of Ponzi to adorn its main lobby in Baltimore, Maryland!

The only difference between Social Security and Ponzi's scheme is that Social Security is much larger (involving a whole country) and was implemented by force. At least Ponzi didn't put a gun to anyone's head and force them to give him their money. And, like all Ponzi-type schemes, Social Security did allow some winners in the beginning; but, in the end, it, too, must collapse, leaving disappointment and heartache in its wake. Three or four generations of Americans will simply lose what two or three other generations might have gained and what was skimmed off by the plan's promoters — the Washington Bureaucracy.

The political con artisits who pulled off and participated in this swindle must be punished. It is to this end that this book is also dedicated.

# 1

# Socialism Arrives in America

Social Security, a program that sprang from the womb of socialism is nothing more than a grotesque economic and social abortion. Like Socialism itself, it owes its very existence to public ignorance and gullibility. Both are swindles on every level — economic, social, moral and legal. The government has consistently misrepresented every aspect of Social Security to the public so Americans have *absolutely no conception* of an item in the Federal budget that accounts for 30% of the government's expenditures. The implication of this is staggering: *better than 99% of Americans do not know anything about a program that consumes as much in taxes as does defense spending!*

Social Security is an economic fraud. It is not supported by even *one* sound economic principle; but, rather, is rooted in the pie-in-the-sky concepts of socialism and the chain letter. As such, it has constantly lowered the nation's standard of living.

It is a fraud on the social level since it actually breeds, aggravates and intensifies all of society's social problems (i.e. creating a less self-reliant population, promoting crime, juvenile delinquency, dependency and unemployment). In effect, Social Security creates and breeds social *insecurity,* the exact opposite of its grandiose, presumptuous, self-serving and misleading title. In addition, the government has totally misrepresented its legal and financial character. What the public has been fed is a complete fairy tale — totally at odds with the real financial and legal nature of the program. However, when we face the fraudulent and illegal character of Social Security, we are brought face to face with what must be the fraudulent character of the Federal judiciary. Without the help of a fraudulent judiciary, the government could *never* have foisted such an illegal program on the public.

Social Security's early advocates and promoters merely adopted the simplistic (but politically salable) economic nostrums of socialism, a common characteristic of much of what was passed off as "New Deal", "Fair Deal", "Great Society" and "New Frontier" programs. Variations of basic socialist doctrine were successfully peddled to the American public under the guise of "liberalism" and the "welfare state", a supposedly benevolent form of free enterprise. In reality, though, the "welfare state" is nothing but socialism disguised and peddled to the public under a more acceptable label.

Politicians generally, of course, love to believe the social and economic philosophies espoused by left-wing intellectuals,[1] since such philosophy fits right in with campaign rhetoric. Politicians love to promise the public that they (the politicians) can wipe out poverty, raise

[1] Actually a contradiction of terms since no real intellectual could possibly accept the absurd and unworkable theories of socialism. Those who embrace such theories are not really intellectuals; they are usually social and economic *theoreticians* (either being too lazy to work or lacking in the ability to create real goods) who, for obvious psychological reasons, reject the economic theory that rewards hard work, creativity and risk taking in favor of one that compensates non-producers and economic cowards (which they invariably are) out of all proportion to their economic and social worth.

living standards, lower rents and interest rates, reduce unemployment, save jobs, "make war on poverty", etc. They promise to do all of this without increasing taxes or requiring anyone to work harder or longer. Unfortunately, all too many are gullible enough to believe this — that politicians, who themselves produce nothing, can increase society's real wealth with laws and economic mirrors. Government all too often fills the need of those who must cling to a belief in Santa Claus.

But our nation's sorry crop of politicians don't raise society's standard of living — they lower it. All they do is pass laws that confiscate the wealth of some (in the guise of taxation) for the benefit of others, in exchange for votes. In the process, these politicians *do* earn considerable sums (and fringe benefits) for themselves ... which is why they go into politics in the first place.[2]

The majority of successful politicians are usually lawyers. Can you think of *any* segment of society less productive than lawyers?[3] In the final analysis it can be said that government today largely consists of a bunch of lawyers passing largely unnecessary laws which (though interfering with society's real producers) do generate a lot of lucrative legal work and influence

[2] It has also been my observation that the least productive members of society go into politics. Picture an individual who is hard working, creative, inventive with a lot of integrity. Ask yourself, "Does such a person go into politics?" Of course not! There might be some exceptions to this, but not many.

[3] I am not saying that society does not need some *good* lawyers, especially where criminal law and Constitutional rights are concerned. But it is my experience that most lawyers are incompetent and overpriced, with a good deal of their work being largely unnecessary. In addition, 75% of the world's lawyers practice in America ... this, alone, proves my point. Incidentally, America has 20 times as many lawyers per capita as Japan, which alone explains Japan's increasing ability to out-produce the U.S. in the area of consumer products.

peddling for them and their cronies in the bar association.[4]

America's founding fathers, fully aware of the type of tyranny that governments are capable of, created a Constitution and a Bill of Rights to limit the power of government so as to prevent such tyrannies from taking place. Federal judges were appointed for life to keep them (theoretically) honest and independent so they would conscientiously enforce this Constitution and the rights secured under it to the public. The Federal judiciary, however, being a part of the Federal government itself, disregarded this trust and continually used its position to illegally expand the power and influence of the Federal government while under-mining individual rights and state sovereignty.[5]

## Social Security Must Lower the Nation's Standard of Living

It is a fundamental economic law that any society will get less of what it taxes and more of what it subsidizes. This principle is so basic that it qualifies as a truism. Let me explain how it works. If a government,

[4] Since licensed lawyers are "officers of the court" all lawyers are automatically a part of the judicial branch of government. Thus, all licensed lawyers who serve in any legislature or executive capacity are automatically a part of two branches of government (legislative and judicial or executive and judicial) at the same time. Such a situation violates the "separation of powers" doctrine. Citizens in every state should seek to bar licensed lawyers from the other two branches of government unless they surrender their bar licenses. Otherwise, not only does such a situation violate the "separation of powers" doctrine, it violates the Constitutional provision outlawing the establishment of a "nobility". Ordinary Americans who are not lawyers are denied access to the judicial branch of government and can only serve in *two* branches of government while *lawyers can serve in all three* - and two of them at the same time! This constitutes a form of "nobility" that is barred by the Constitution.

for example, placed a tax of $100.00 per year on "playing tennis", fewer people would play tennis. To some, playing tennis would not be worth $100.00 per year. If the "tennis playing" tax were raised to $200.00 per year, society would get fewer tennis players still. If the tax on "tennis playing" was increased further we would obviously get even fewer tennis players. And, if the tax were raised high enough, we could conceivably wipe out tennis playing altogether![6] Social Security (which you will soon learn is simply another "income" tax) is a tax on *productivity* since only those who are productive (i.e. working) are taxed. So, if government taxes "productivity", society must (in conformity with economic law) get less of it.

The collateral principle, that a society "will get more of what it subsidizes", is also a truism. For example, if our government stated that it would pay an annual subsidy of $100.00 to anyone who played tennis, some people would now play tennis for the $100.00 subsidy. The nation would suddenly find it had more tennis players. If the government raised the "tennis" subsidy to $200.00 per year, we would obviously get more tennis players still. And, if the government raised the subsidy high enough, everybody in the country who could make it to a tennis court would be playing tennis!

Since all Social Security "benefits" are tied to "not working" or working less, Social Security payments amount to a government subsidy for "not working" and,

[5] The 10th Amendment was specifically designed to protect and secure individual rights and state sovereignty. It states, "...those powers not delegated to the United States by the Constitution nor prohibited to it by the States, are reserved to the States respectively or to the people."

[6] Or, as was succinctly put by Chief Justice John Marshall, "The power to tax involves the power to destroy." *(McCulloch v. Maryland,* 4 Wheat. 316 (1819)

in turn, America gets a lot more "non-workers" because of it. Since Social Security amounts to a tax on "productivity" and a subsidy for "non-productivity", the existence of such a program delivers a two-fold blow to the nation's economy. The nation gets fewer producers and more non-producers, which *has to lower the nation's standard of living and quality of life.*

The government succeeded in selling such an idiotic plan to the nation because thousands of Federal politicians and bureaucrats have been thoroughly misstating and misrepresenting Social Security to the public.

It has also received a lot of help over the years from supposed "experts" who have been feeding the public a lot of nonsense concerning Social Security. Examples of such nonsense are included in Appendix D.

So let's cut through all the nonsense, find out what Social Security *really* is, and discover how anyone can drop out.

## SUMMARIZING THE POINTS COVERED IN CHAPTER 1

1. Social Security is rooted in Socialist doctrine.
2. Social Security (being a tax on producers for the benefit of non-producers) must decrease the number of producers while increasing the number of non-producers.
3. The inevitable result of 2 above is a continual lowering of the nation's standard of living.

# 2

# *Surprise! Social Security-Just Another "Income" Tax*

Reproduced in Figure 1 is the Internal Revenue Code section that establishes the present, basic 5.4% rate for "Social Security". Figure 2 is the Code section that *presumably* establishes the supplemental 1.3% rate for "medicaid", which equals the current 6.7% "Social Security" tax withheld from wages.

Note that Chapter 21 of the Code is specifically entitled *Federal Insurance Contributions Act* while sections 3101(a) and 3101(b) are respectively captioned "Old Age, Survivors and Disability Insurance" and "Hospital Insurance". Read over both Code sections and see what impression you get. After reading them, did you conclude that they deal with taxes for "hospital insurance" and/ or "old age and disability insurance"? Read them again and see if either section deals with any such programs!

First of all, *chapter titles and section headings do not constitute a part of the law,* but the public would not know this when reading the Code. Both the Chapter Title and Code captions used here are deliberately designed to fool the public as to what the law actually is.

## FIGURE 1

### CHAPTER 21.—FEDERAL INSURANCE CONTRIBUTIONS ACT

**Chapter Title**

Subchapter
A. Tax on employees.
B. Tax on employers.
C. General provisions.

#### Subchapter A.—Tax on Employees

Sec.
3101. Rate of tax.
3102. Deduction of tax from wages.

**Sec. 3101. Rate of tax.**

**Section Heading**

**(a) Old-age, survivors, and disability insurance.**

In addition to other taxes, there is hereby imposed on the income of every individual a tax equal to the following percentages of the wages (as defined in section 3121(a)) received by him with respect to employment (as defined in section 3121(b))—

**(1)** with respect to wages received during the calendar years 1974 through 1977, the rate shall be 4.95 percent;
**(2)** with respect to wages received during the calendar year 1978, the rate shall be 5.05 percent;
**(3)** with respect to wages received during the calendar years 1979 and 1980, the rate shall be 5.08 percent;
**(4)** with respect to wages received during the calendar year 1981, the rate shall be 5.35 percent;
**(5)** with respect to wages received during the calendar years 1982 through 1984, the rate shall be 5.40 percent;
**(6)** with respect to wages received during the calendar years 1985 through 1989, the rate shall be 5.70 percent; and
**(7)** with respect to wages received after December 31, 1989, the rate shall be 6.20 percent.

## FIGURE 2

**Code Sec. 3101**

**Section Heading**

**(b) Hospital insurance.**

In addition to the tax imposed by the preceding subsection, there is hereby imposed on the income of every individual a tax equal to the following percentages of the wages (as defined in section 3121(a)) received by him with respect to employment (as defined in section 3121(b))—

**(1)** with respect to wages received during the calendar years 1974 through 1977, the rate shall be 0.90 percent;

**(2)** with respect to wages received during the calendar year 1978, the rate shall be 1.00 percent;

**(3)** with respect to wages received during the calendar years 1979 and 1980, the rate shall be 1.05 percent;

**(4)** with respect to wages received during the calendar years 1981 through 1984, the rate shall be 1.30 percent;

**(5)** with respect to wages received during the calendar year 1985, the rate shall be 1.35 percent; and

**(6)** with respect to wages received after December 31, 1985, the rate shall be 1.45 percent.

For example, the Chapter title, "Federal Insurance Contributions Act", is, itself, a lie. As explained in Appendix A "Social Security" is not "insurance", and, in any case, it is supported by *forced exactions* – not *voluntary "contributions"*.

The paragraph subheadings are also deliberately designed to carry out the misleading idea that somehow the law deals with "contributions" for these "insurance" benefits, when this is not at all the case. You can prove this yourself by placing your finger over the caption headings and reading the law as written. You will discover that *there is nothing in the law that even mentions* old age, disability, survivors or hospital insurance benefits at all! So, if the law itself does not mention these subjects, how can the captions (which are *not* part of the law) refer to them?! Obviously the captions were designed to (mis)lead the public concerning what the law itself is all about. The fact is, if the law really contained the material suggested by those captions, "Social Security" would have been declared unconstitutional a long time ago![1]

By reading the law (and forgetting the captions), you will quickly discover what has been going on — which is something entirely different from what the nation has been led to believe.

First of all, the public believes that "Social Security" is a tax on "wages". But as you can see from the law, *"Social Security" is really nothing more than another "income" tax!* American wage earners have been paying *two* "income" taxes — one collected on the basis of a form 1040 (subject to deductions and exemptions) and another (a flat rate "income" tax automatically deducted from wages) not subject to such deductions or exemptions! Can the Federal government make some Americans subject to two "income" taxes while excluding others (such as retirees and government employees) from the same tax?? Surely not!

It is important to note that the "income" tax established in Code section 3101 is merely "collected as a percentage of wages", but the tax itself is clearly identi-

[1] See page 81.

fied as an "income" tax and *not a tax on wages!* It is possible to have *wages* but not *income,* since "income" (as used in the 16th Amendment) is a legal concept separate and distinct from wages![2] As a matter of fact, the word "wages" is not even included in Code section 61 which *attempts* to define the components of "income" (Figure 8, page 33). The point is, though your employer may have evidence that you received "wages", he has no knowledge or evidence (unless you tell him) as to whether or not you have any "income". And the law imposes no obligation on employers to determine whether their employees have "income". The government *could not* impose such a burden on employers because it would amount to the government forcing employers to be detectives for them. In addition, the "income" tax imposed under section 3101 cannot be legally collected until it has been lawfully assessed by the government in accordance with section 6201 of the Internal Revenue Code as shown in Figure 3.

## Government Required to Assess and Bill "Social Security" Taxes

Note that Code section 6201 requires that the Secretary of the Treasury make an assessment "of all taxes . . . imposed by this title". Since section 3101 clearly imposes an "income" tax, then such taxes are *required to be assessed* in accordance with Section 6201. In addition, Section 6203 (Figure 4) states that the assessment shall be made by recording the "liability" of the taxpayer "in the office of the Secretary"; and that "upon request of the taxpayer the Secretary shall furnish the taxpayer with a copy of the record of the assessment". In addition, Section 6303 (Figure 5) states that

[2] For a more complete analysis, see chapter 3.

## FIGURE 3

**Sec. 6201. Assessment authority.**

**(a) Authority of Secretary.**

The Secretary is authorized and required to make the inquiries, determinations, and assessments of all taxes (including interest, additional amounts, additions to the tax, and assessable penalties) imposed by this title, or accruing under any former internal revenue law, which have not been duly paid by stamp at the time and in the manner provided by law. Such authority shall extend to and include the following:

**(1) Taxes shown on return.** The Secretary shall assess all taxes determined by the taxpayer or by the Secretary as to which returns or lists are made under this title.

## FIGURE 4

**Sec. 6203. Method of assessment.**

The assessment shall be made by recording the liability of the taxpayer in the office of the Secretary in accordance with rules or regulations prescribed by the Secretary. Upon request of the taxpayer, the Secretary shall furnish the taxpayer a copy of the record of the assessment.

**FIGURE 5**

**Sec. 6303. Notice and demand for tax.**

**(a) General rule.**

Where it is not otherwise provided by this title, the Secretary shall, as soon as practicable, and within 60 days, after the making of an assessment of a tax pursuant to section 6203, give notice to each person liable for the unpaid tax, stating the amount and demanding payment thereof. Such notice shall be left at the dwelling or usual place of business of such person, or shall be sent by mail to such person's last known address.

after making the assessment the Secretary shall "... give notice to each person liable for the unpaid tax, stating the amount and demanding payment thereof." I, therefore, suggest that you send the letter shown in Figure 6 to the Secretary of the Treasury to determine whether Section 3101 "income" taxes have been properly assessed against you, since without such an assessment you obviously have no "liability" for such taxes!

## Can Americans Have Two Types Of "Income"?

What "income" is actually subject to tax under Section 3101 anyway? Can employees have *two different* kinds of "income"? Obviously the "income" that Americans pay taxes on using a form 1040 is entirely different from the "income" that has served as a basis for the taxes that have been forceably extracted from paychecks pursuant to Section 3101.

When determining 1040 "income", employees are allowed numerous deductions and exemptions and may ultimately arrive at a taxable "income" substantially lower than their wages. Can employees legally have

## FIGURE 6

Mr. Donald T. Regan, Secretary
Department of the Treasury
Main Treasury Building
15th Street & Pennsylvania Avenue, N. W.
Washington, D.C. 20220

Dear Mr. Secretary:

Section 6201 of the IRS Code states that you are "required to make the . . . assessments of all taxes . . . imposed by this title". Section 6203 further states that the assessment shall be made by "recording the liability of the taxpayer in the office of the Secretary" and "upon request of the taxpayer, the Secretary shall furnish the taxpayer with the record of the assessment".

This is to advise you that I would like to be furnished a copy of the record of my tax assessment (pursuant to Sections 6201 and 6203) for any "income" taxes for which I may be liable for under Sections 3101(a) and (b) of the Internal Revenue Code. Please furnish me with my current 1984 assessment and a copy of the assessment for the years 1983, 1982, 1981, 1980, etc.

I also note that Section 6303 of the IRS Code states that the Secretary shall "within 60 days after the making of an assessment pursuant to Section 6203, give notice to each person liable for the unpaid tax, stating the amount and demanding payment thereof".

This is to inform you that I am notifying my employer that until such time as I receive from you a copy of my record of assessment for the current year, and proof that I have been "made liable" for Section 3101 "income" taxes pursuant to Sections 6201, 6203 and 6303, he is to immediately stop the withholding of all such "income" taxes from my wages.

Very truly yours,

Ima Freeman

two different kinds of taxable "income"? One being taxable *one way* under section 3101 and another kind being taxable *another way* on a form 1040?[3] Does the 16th Amendment provide for *two different* kinds of "income" that are taxable pursuant to that Amendment?

## Internal Revenue Code Does Not Define "Income"

Figure 7 is an excerpt from the case of *U.S. vs. Ballard* in which the Appellate court clearly recognized that ". . . the general term 'income' is not defined in the Internal Revenue Code." Well, if the general term "income" is not defined in the Internal Revenue Code, how can anyone be sure that they have any "income" that is taxable? You will notice that the court in *Ballard* states that Section 61 of the Code defines "gross income". I have reproduced Code Section 61 (Figure 8) and you will see that the Court is wrong on this point — Code Section 61 *does not* define "gross income" at all. Code Section 61 *attempts* to define "gross income" but uses the word "income" in the definition and (as any eighth grader should know) a word cannot be defined by using the word itself in the definition! In other words, Code Section 61 cannot define "gross income" unless the word "income" is also defined.[4] But even overlooking this piece of chicanery, Section 61 (Figure 8) admittedly only defines "*gross* income". In the same manner, Code Section 62 (Figure 9) defines "*adjusted* gross income",

[3] Regular income taxes on a form 1040 are "imposed" in Section 1 of the Internal Revenue Code. It states that ". . . there is hereby imposed on . . . taxable income . . . a tax determined in accordance with the following tables. . ."

[4] For a more complete analysis, see *Why No One Can Have Taxable Income by* Irwin Schiff, to be published in 1984.

## FIGURE 7

### U.S. v. Ballard, 535 F 2nd 499

**535 FEDERAL REPORTER, 2d SERIES**

The general term "income" is not defined in the Internal Revenue Code. Section 61 of the Code, 26 U.S.C. § 61, defines "gross income" to mean

> all income from whatever source derived, including (but not limited to) the following items:
>
> (1) Compensation for services, including fees, commissions, and similar items;
>
> (2) Gross income derived from business;
>
> * * * * * *
>
> (5) Rents [.]
>
> * * * * * *

while Code Section 63 (Figure 10) allegedly defines "*taxable* income".

For the reason already stated, neither Code Section 62 nor 63 actually defines "adjusted" or "taxable" income either. But, admittedly, no section of the Code even *attempts* to define the naked word "income" and it is naked "income" that is allegedly taxed in Code Sec-

## FIGURE 8

**Sec. 61. Gross income defined.**

**(a) General definition.**

Except as otherwise provided in this subtitle, gross income means all income from whatever source derived, including (but not limited to) the following items:

(1) Compensation for services, including fees, commissions, and similar items;

(2) Gross income derived from business;

(3) Gains derived from dealings in property;

(4) Interest;

(5) Rents;

(6) Royalties;

(7) Dividends;

(8) Alimony and separate maintenance payments;

(9) Annuities;

(10) Income from life insurance and endowment contracts;

(11) Pensions;

(12) Income from discharge of indebtedness;

(13) Distributive share of partnership gross income;

(14) Income in respect of a decedent; and

(15) Income from an interest in an estate or trust.

* Note that Section (a) does not include either "wages" or "salaries" as a component of "Gross Income." This omission was *not accidental*. The government, however, has suceeded in tricking the public into believing that "wages" and "salaries" are "similar items" to "compensation for services", "fees", and "commissions." They are not. A corporation, for example, can receive "compensation for services" as well as "fees" and "commissions," but it cannot receive "wages" or a salary. So wages and salaries *are not* similar to the items listed in (a) (1) and thus they can not be legally included in "gross income" or any other kind of "income".

## FIGURE 9

**Sec. 63. Taxable income defined.**

**(a) Corporations.**

For purposes of this subtitle, in the case of a corporation, the term "taxable income" means gross income minus the deductions allowed by this chapter.

**(b) Individuals.**

For purposes of this subtitle, in the case of an individual, the term "taxable income" means adjusted gross income—

(1) reduced by the sum of—

(A) the excess itemized deductions,

(B) the deductions for personal exemptions provided by section 151, and

(C) the direct charitable deduction, and

(2) increased (in the case of an individual for whom an unused zero bracket amount computation is provided by subsection (e)) by the unused zero bracket amount (if any).

## FIGURE 10

**Sec. 62. Adjusted gross income defined.**

For purposes of this subtitle, the term "adjusted gross income" means, in the case of an individual, gross income minus the following deductions:

tion 3101![5] But, if "income" is nowhere defined in the Internal Revenue Code, how can "income" be logically or legally taxed? Can a law tax something that the law does not define? Remember, "income" as such, does not exist. It is an abstract term. Try to take a picture of "income". Since it does not exist in concrete form (as do other taxable commodities such as cigars, cigarettes, beer, wine, gasoline, etc.), it *must* be clearly defined or *it cannot be taxed*! Since nowhere in the Code is "income" defined, "income" as used in Section 6103 obviously cannot be taxed *on any basis*; or as the courts would say:

> "Nothing is taxable unless clearly within a taxing statute." (*BENTE vs BUGBEE* 103 NJL 608)
>
> "Any doubt as to the persons or property intended to be included in a tax statute will be resolved in favor of the taxpayer." (*MILLER vs ILLINOIS C.R. CO.* 146 Miss 422)

Pursuing this argument further (which amounts to beating a dead horse), "income" as used in Section 3101 cannot logically be different from "income" as defined in Section 63; and taxes on such "income" cannot be deducted automatically from wages without taking into consideration all the deductions and allowances provided by Section 63. If it *is* automatically deducted, this makes the tax a *direct* tax on "wages" instead of a tax on "income". Remember, the *income* tax "imposed" in section 3101 is merely *collected* as a percentage of *wages* and is not a tax *on* wages but a tax *on* "income".

[5] You will ultimately discover that no one can have "income" that is taxable either as a "Social Security" tax or as a regular "income" tax. But for now I merely want to demonstrate that no one can have "income" that is taxable under Section 3101 apart from any other consideration and overlooking entirely that "income" itself cannot be the subject of an *enforced* tax *on any basis*!

## SUMMARIZING THE POINTS IN CHAPTER 2

1. Social Security taxes withheld from employee wages are "income" taxes and not taxes on wages.
2. Since the Internal Revenue Code does not define "income", no one can have "income" that can be subject to section 3101 "income" taxes.
3. No employer can know whether an employee has "income" subject to tax under Section 3101, nor is any employer authorized or required to make such a determination.
4. In any case, Section 6201 of the Internal Revenue Code requires that the Secretary of the Treasury assess Section 3101 "income" taxes.
5. Section 6203 further requires that the Secretary of the Treasury record an employee's Section 3101 "income" tax liability and furnish the employee a copy of that record of assessment if so requested by the employee; and
6. Code Section 6303 requires the government to send a tax bill to each employee for any Section 3101 "income" taxes for which he may be "liable". Until employees receive such a bill they can have no Section 3101 "income" tax liability!
7. It is obviously unconstitutional for the government to impose two "income" taxes on some Americans while millions of government employees and other citizens are subject to just one.

8. There is nothing in the Internal Revenue Code that requires taxes collected as "Social Security" taxes to be earmarked *in any way* for supposed "Social Security" purposes.

# 3

# How To Stop Employers From Withholding "Social Security" Taxes

To stop your employer from deducting an undefined and unassessed "income" tax from your wages, simply give him the affidavit shown in Figure 11. When you give your employer a sworn affidavit stating that you have no "income" that is taxable under Section 3101, he has *no choice* but to stop deducting such "income" taxes from your wages.

Employers are only authorized (under Section 3101) to deduct "income" taxes from employee wages. If an employee certifies that he has no "income" the employer has no legal basis for deducting "Social Security" taxes! Employers who, nevertherless, continue deducting these taxes (despite having no proof or a court order to the contrary) are liable to the employee for such arbitrary, unauthorized and unwarranted deductions.

## Employers Subject to Lawsuits

If your employer does not immediately stop withholding Section 3101 "income" taxes from your wages

## FIGURE 11

### AFFIDAVIT

1. I, ________________, swear under the penalty of perjury that I have no income that is taxable under 26 U.S.C. 3101.
2. I have never been made liable for any such tax pursuant to 26 U.S.C. 6201.
3. I have never received a copy of any assessment for any such tax, pursuant to 26 U.S.C. 6203.
4. I received no notice of any liability for any such tax, pursuant to 26 U.S.C. 6303.
5. Therefore, you have no legal basis for withholding any "income" taxes (allegedly imposed by 26 U.S.C. 3101) from my wages.
6. I understand that you will rely upon this affidavit in making your determination not to withhold from my wages any taxes imposed pursuant to 26 U.S.C. 3101.

______________________________
Signature

______________________________
Date

______________________________
Notary

______________________________
My Commission Expires

Attached Exhibits ______________________________

* Note: See Appendix C for letter that accompanies this affidavit.

(after you send him your affidavit), you should immediately notify him that you are going to sue him[1] for any portion of your wages that he has illegally withheld (or continues to withhold) and sends to the government. Remember, he would be sending the government a portion of your wages for a tax which, by law, you could not possibly owe or be liable for.

The government, however, anticipated that some employees might see through their illegal scam, and would threaten employers with such lawsuits, so they tried to cover this contingency by including Section 3102(b) (see Figure 12) in the Code.

## FIGURE 12

**Sec. 3102. Deduction of tax from wages.**

**(b) Indemnification of employer.**

Every employer required so to deduct the tax shall be liable for the payment of such tax, and shall be indemnified against the claims and demands of any person for the amount of any such payment made by such employer.

It is a very interesting section of "law", which states that employers ". . . shall be indemnified against the claims and demands of any person for the amount of any such payment made by such employer." When employers are notified of impending lawsuits they should send the letter shown in Figure 13 to the government. If the government does not respond to this letter by

[1] See Appendix C for sample lawsuit.

agreeing to defend and indemnify the employer, then the employer is obviously free to *immediately* stop withholding Section 3101 "income taxes. Can the government *force* employers to expose themselves to such lawsuits (by forcing them to withhold money from employee paychecks) without any assurance that they will be defended and indemnified?

## Section 3102 — Legal Fiction

Actually, Section 3102(b) is based on fraud (designed to give employers a false sense of security) since it only promises to indemnify employers "required" to deduct Section 3101 "income" taxes. Since *no* employer is "required" to deduct such taxes, this section cannot apply to any employer! Section 3102(a) (Figure 14) is the Code section dealing with the deduction of such taxes and makes this abundantly clear.

You will note that nowhere in Section 3102(a) does it state that any employer is "required" to deduct Section 3101 "income" taxes. The section merely states that such taxes ". . . *shall* be collected . . .". The Federal government relies on the public confusing "shall" with "required". In these tax statutes, however, the word "shall" actually means "may" and, the word "may" can be used in place of "shall", making the above statement read that employers "*may* collect" such taxes[2].

In any case, the word "shall" appears in this Section only once while the word "may" appears four times

[2] For example, the Supreme Court held in *Cairo Fulton RR vs. Hecht* 95 U.S. 170 that ". . . as against the government the word shall when used in statutes is to be construed as "may" unless a contrary intention is manifested." For a more detailed explanation of this, see pages 34–37 of *How Anyone Can Stop Paying Income Taxes by* Irwin Schiff (Hamden, CT: Freedom Books, 1982).

## FIGURE 13

Mr. Donald T. Regan
Secretary of the Treasury
Main Treasury Building
15th Street & Pennsylvania Avenue, N.W.
Washington, D.C. 20220

Dear Mr. Secretary:

I have been threatened with a lawsuit by my employee ______________________________ if I remove any "income" taxes from his/her wages as imposed by 26 U.S.C. 3101.

Attached is his/her affidavit swearing that he/she has no income subject to such tax and further that he/she has never been notified by the government that such a tax was ever assessed or recorded. He/she also swears that he/she has never received any notice of "liability" for such a tax pursuant to 26 U.S.C., Sections 6201, 6203 and 6303.

Not wishing to expose myself to any liability in this matter, I will no longer withhold such taxes from ____________________'s wages until you notify me in writing that the government will pay any and all costs of litigation and will indemnify me against all claims and losses I might incur (pursuant to 26 U.S.C. 3102[b] should I disregard his/her sworn statement.

Very truly yours,

Fred Hardnose
President

## FIGURE 14

**Sec. 3102. Deduction of tax from wages.**

**(a) Requirement.**

The tax imposed by section 3101 shall be collected by the employer of the taxpayer, by deducting the amount of the tax from the wages as and when paid. An employer who in any calendar quarter pays to an employee cash remuneration to which paragraph (7)(B) of section 3121(a) is applicable may deduct an amount equivalent to such tax from any such payment of remuneration, even though at the time of payment the total amount of such remuneration paid to the employee by the employer in the calendar quarter is less than $50; and an employer who in any calendar year pays to an employee cash remuneration to which paragraph (7)(C) or (10) of section 3121(a) is applicable may deduct an amount equivalent to such tax from any such payments of remuneration, even though at the time of payment the total amount of such remuneration paid to the employee by the employer in the calendar year is less than $100; and an employer who in any calendar year pays to an employee cash remuneration to which paragraph (8)(B) of section 3121(a) is applicable may deduct an amount equivalent to such tax from any such payment of remuneration, even though at the time of payment the total amount of such remuneration paid to the employee by the employer in the calendar year is less than $150 and the employee has not performed agricultural labor for the employer on 20 days or more in the calendar year for cash remuneration computed on a time basis; and an employer who is furnished by an employee a written statement of tips (received in a calendar month) pursuant to section 6053(a) to which paragraph (12)(B) of section 3121(a) is applicable may deduct an amount equivalent to such tax with respect to such tips from any wages of the employee (exclusive of tips) under his control, even though at the time such statement is furnished the total amount of the tips included in statements furnished to the employer as having been received by the employee in such calendar month in the course of his employment by such employer is less than $20.

and the word "required" does not appear at all! This is no accident. Employers cannot (constitutionally) be forced to be unpaid tax collectors for the government. Such a requirement would render the law unconstitutional since it would violate the 13th Amendment of the U.S. Constitution (which outlaws *involuntary servitude*). In addition, the government certainly could not compound the illegality by forcing such unpaid tax collectors to further expose themselves to employee lawsuits! Thus, Section 3102(b) is a legal fiction because the government is only authorized to indemnify "employers *required* to deduct". Since Section 3102 *does not* impose such a *requirement* or *obligation* on any employer, the government is actually barred by law from indemnifying any employer sued by an employee for illegally withholding Section 3101 "income" taxes. And, further, since employers cannot be forced to expose themselves to lawsuits for which they *cannot* receive indemnification, they should immediately cease withholding such taxes. Of course, any employer can stop deducting anyway, since (as you can see) the law *does not* impose a withholding requirement! Section 3102(b) does, however, attempt to further trick employers into believing that they can be "liable" for taxes not withheld. But note such a "liability" only extends to employers "required" to deduct and since no employer is "required" to deduct, no employer can be "liable" for the taxes not deducted!

## SUMMARIZING THE POINTS COVERED IN CHAPTER 3

1. There is no law that "requires" employers to withhold Section 3101 "income" taxes from employee wages.

2. Supplying a sworn statement to one's employer (certifying that one has no "income" that is taxable under Section 3101) furnishes a legal bar from having such taxes taken from one's pay.
3. Employers withholding Section 3101 "income" taxes from the wages of an employee (after being notified that said employee has no "income" tax liability under Section 3101) can be liable to such employee for any wages illegally withheld and sent to the government.
4. The law bars the government from indemnifying those employers who are sued by their employees for illegally withholding 3101 "income" taxes from their wages.

# 4

# Employers and Self-Employeds – How They, Too, Can Drop Out

As explained (see page 221, *Appendix A*), it is the employees who actually pay *both* portions of "Social Security" taxes. With that in mind let's examine that portion of the tax theoretically paid by the employer per Code Section 3111(a) and (b) (Figure 15). Note again the misleading captions, but also note these important differences:

1. First, the tax on the employer is specifically identified as being an "excise" tax. This clearly establishes that the tax on employees is an *unapportioned, direct tax* and, therefore, *automatically unconstitutional.*[1]
2. Both Section 3101(a) and (b) clearly show that the taxes they impose are taxes on *wages*. Note neither section even mentions "income".

This, of course, confirms the fact that Section 3101 taxes are "income" taxes (illegally levied as a direct

[1] See *Why No One Can Have Taxable Income* by Irwin Schiff.

**Subchapter B.—Tax on Employers**

**Sec. 3111. Rate of tax.**

**(a) Old-age, survivors, and disability insurance.**

In addition to other taxes, there is hereby imposed on every employer an excise tax, with respect to having individuals in his employ, equal to the following percentages of the wages (as defined in section 3121(a) and (t)) paid by him with respect to employment (as defined in section 3121(b))—

**(1)** with respect to wages paid during the calendar years 1974 through 1977, the rate shall be 4.95 percent;

**(2)** with respect to wages paid during the calendar year 1978, the rate shall be 5.05 percent;

**(3)** with respect to wages paid during the calendar years 1979 and 1980, the rate shall be 5.08 percent;

**(4)** with respect to wages paid during the calendar year 1981, the rate shall be 5.35 percent;

**(5)** with respect to wages paid during the calendar years 1982 through 1984, the rate shall be 5.40 percent;

**(6)** with respect to wages paid during the calendar years 1985 through 1989, the rate shall be 5.70 percent; and

**(7)** with respect to wages paid after December 31, 1989, the rate shall be 6.20 percent.

**(b) Hospital insurance.**

In addition to the tax imposed by the preceding subsection, there is hereby imposed on every employer an excise tax, with respect to having individuals in his employ, equal to the following percentages of the wages (as defined in section 3121(a) and (t)) paid by him with respect to employment (as defined in section 3121(b))—

**(1)** with respect to wages paid during the calendar years 1974 through 1977, the rate shall be 0.90 percent;

**(2)** with respect to wages paid during the calendar year 1978, the rate shall be 1.00 percent;

**(3)** with respect to wages paid during the calendar years 1979 and 1980, the rate shall be 1.05 percent;

**(4)** with respect to wages paid during the calendar years 1981 through 1984, the rate shall be 1.30 percent;

**(5)** with respect to wages paid during the calendar year 1985, the rate shall be 1.35 percent; and

**(6)** with respect to wages paid after December 31, 1985, the rate shall be 1.45 percent.

**FIGURE 15**

tax) as compared to Section 3111 which creates a contrived excise tax, levied "with respect to having individuals in (your) employ equal to a percentage of the wages paid".

The tax is a *contrived* excise because it is not levied *on* anything — not a product or even a supposed privilege. Excise taxes are levied *on* things (i.e. *on* a bottle of wine, *on* a pack of cigarettes, *on* a gallon of gas or, as in the case of Federal estate or gift taxes, *on* the supposed privilege of bequeathing or giving away property). The fact that this tax is being levied "with respect to having individuals in (one's) employ" is proof that the tax is not a legitimate excise since it is not levied *on* anything, and cannot be an excise tax within the meaning of the U.S. Constitution! Its use here merely signals the government's attempt to jimmy an unauthorized tax into Article 1, Section 8, Paragraph 1 of the Constitution. That the attempt was, indeed, fraudulent was pointed out by the First Circuit Court of Appeals when it found Social Security unconstitutional on this and other grounds (see pages 68-70).

But, in any case, it should be noted that the tax itself was to be determined by wages and not by income. So the employee tax is clearly a tax on income as opposed to the employer's portion which is a tax on nothing, but measured by employee wages.[2]

## Do Employers Have to Pay The Tax?

The employer's "excise" tax is the only tax created by the Social Security Act for which some legitimacy

[2] Actually, both taxes are unconstitutional "capitation" taxes. One being measured by wages received and the other measured by wages paid out. For an explanation as to why both capitation taxes are illegal, see Irwin Schiff's *Why No One Can Have Taxable Income.*

might *conceivably* be claimed. This is because 1) the tax itself does not claim to be a tax on "income"; 2) the law clearly identifies the tax as an *excise* tax; 3) the Federal government can levy excise taxes without being restricted by the apportionment provisions the Constitution imposes on direct taxes; and 4) the Supreme Court has held (albeit incorrectly) that the tax is a valid excise. Despite these factors, however, there are a number of legal grounds for not paying the tax.

*Social Security Act is Admittedly Repugnant To The Constitution*

Since it is a fundamental principal of American jurisprudence that "anything repugnant to the Constitution is null and void" (*Marbury* vs. *Madison* 1 CR. 137), it can be argued that since the Social Security Act is admittedly unconstitutional (see pages 85-89) all taxes created under it are, therefore, null and void.

*Since Employers Are Not Taxed "For The General Welfare of The U.S.", The Tax is Admittedly Illegal*

As explained in Chapter 5, the government (in arguing Social Security's constitutionality before the Supreme Court) claimed that Social Security taxes were not designed to pay for Social Security benefits, but were "true taxes (their) purposes being simply to raise revenue," (page 81). The Supreme Court (in its 1938 decision) refused to rule on this question stating that it would "leave the question open". So if the question was left open in 1938, the question certainly has been closed by the government since it repeatedly admits that Social Security taxes, (and the numerous increases in them), are needed to pay for Social Security benefits, not "simply to raise revenue". (see Chapter 8)

### *Law Does Not "Require" That The Tax be Paid*

But the most basic reason that employers do not have to pay this "excise" tax is that there is nothing in the law that establishes a "liability" for the tax or any requirement that it be paid! For example, IRS Code Section 5703(a) (Figure 16) clearly states that "The manufacturer or importer of tobacco products and cigarette papers and tubes *shall be liable* for the taxes imposed thereon by Section 5701". Section 5701 (Figure 17) is the Code Section that "imposed" the tax on tobacco products. In addition, Code Section 5703(b) (Figure 18) provides that, "The taxes imposed in Section 5701 shall be paid on the basis of a return". The same wording with respect to the creation of a tax "liability" (and a requirement that such taxes "be paid") appears in numerous other code sections with respect to other Federal taxes. For example, Section 4374 (Figure 19) clearly states that the tax imposed by Section 4371 (Figure 20) "shall be paid on a basis of a return". Since no section of the Internal Revenue Code establishes a "liability", or a requirement that the taxes imposed by Section 3111 "shall be paid", such taxes are, obviously, not *required* to be paid!

## FIGURE 16

### Code Sec. 5703

**Sec. 5703. Liability for tax and method of payment.**

**(a) Liability for tax.**

**(1) Original liability.** The manufacturer or importer of tobacco products and cigarette papers and tubes shall be liable for the taxes imposed thereon by section 5701.

## FIGURE 17

### Code Sec. 5701

**Sec. 5701. Rate of tax.**

**(a) Cigars**

On cigars, manufactured in or imported into the United States, there shall be imposed the following taxes:

(1) **Small cigars.** On cigars, weighing not more than 3 pounds per thousand, 75 cents per thousand;

(2) **Large cigars.** On cigars weighing more than 3 pounds per thousand, a tax equal to 8½ percent of the wholesale price, but not more than $20 per thousand.

Cigars not exempt from tax under this chapter which are removed but not intended for sale shall be taxed at the same rate as similar cigars removed for sale.

**(b) Cigarettes.**

On cigarettes, manufactured in or imported into the United States, there shall be imposed the following taxes:

(1) **Small cigarettes.** On cigarettes, weighing not more than 3 pounds per thousand, $8 per thousand.

(2) **Large cigarettes.** On cigarettes, weighing more than 3 pounds per thousand, $16.80 per thousand; except that, if more than 6½ inches in length, they shall be taxable at the rate prescribed for cigarettes weighing not more than 3 pounds per thousand, counting each 2¾ inches, or fraction thereof, of the length of each as one cigarette.

**(c) Cigarette papers.**

On each book or set of cigarette papers containing more than 25 papers, manufactured in or imported into the United States, there shall be imposed a tax of ½ cent for each 50 papers or fractional part thereof; except that, if cigarette papers measure more than 6½ inches in length, they shall be taxable at the rate prescribed, counting each 2¾ inches, or fraction thereof, of the length of each as one cigarette paper.

**(d) Cigarette tubes.**

On cigarette tubes, manufactured in or imported into the United States, there shall be imposed a tax of 1 cent for each 50 tubes or fractional part thereof, except that if cigarette tubes measure more than 6½ inches in length, they shall be taxable at the rate prescribed, counting each 2¾ inches, or fraction thereof, of the length of each as one cigarette tube.

**(e) Imported tobacco products and cigarette papers and tubes.**

The taxes imposed by this section on tobacco products and cigarette papers and tubes imported into the United States shall be in addition to any import duties imposed on such articles, unless such import duties are imposed in lieu of internal revenue tax.

## FIGURE 18

### Code Sec. 5703

**(b) Method of payment of tax.**

**(1) In general.** The taxes imposed by section 5701 shall be determined at the time of removal of the tobacco products and cigarette papers and tubes. Such taxes shall be paid on the basis of return. The Secretary shall, by regulations, prescribe the period or the event for which such return shall be made and the information to be furnished on such return. Any postponement under this subsection of the payment of taxes determined at the time of removal shall be conditioned upon the filing of such additional bonds, and upon compliance with such requirements, as the Secretary may prescribe for the protection of the revenue. The Secretary may, by regulations, require payment of tax on the basis of a return prior to removal of the tobacco products and cigarette papers and tubes where a person defaults in the postponed payment of tax on the basis of a return under this subsection or regulations prescribed thereunder. All administrative and penalty provisions of this title, insofar as applicable, shall apply to any tax imposed by section 5701.

## FIGURE 19

### Code Sec. 4374

**Sec. 4374. Liability for tax.**

The tax imposed by this chapter shall be paid, on the basis of a return, by any person who makes, signs, issues, or sells any of the documents and instruments subject to the tax, or for whose use or benefit the same are made, signed, issued, or sold. The United States or any agency or instrumentality thereof shall not be liable for the tax.

FIGURE 20

**CHAPTER 34—POLICIES ISSUED BY FOREIGN INSURERS**

Sec.
4371. Imposition of tax.
4372. Definitions.
4373. Exemptions.
4374. Liability for tax.

**Sec. 4371. Imposition of tax.**

There is hereby imposed, on each policy of insurance, indemnity bond, annuity contract, or policy of reinsurance issued by any foreign insurer or reinsurer, a tax at the following rates:

**(1) Casualty insurance and indemnity bonds.** 4 cents on each dollar, or fractional part thereof, of the premium paid on the policy of casualty insurance or the indemnity bond, if issued to or for, or in the name of, an insured as defined in section 4372(d);

**(2) Life insurance, sickness and accident policies, and annuity contracts.** 1 cent on each dollar, or fractional part thereof, of the premium paid on the policy of life, sickness, or accident insurance, or annuity contract, unless the insurer is subject to tax under section 819; and

**(3) Reinsurance.** 1 cent on each dollar, or fractional part thereof, of the premium paid on the policy of reinsurance covering any of the contracts taxable under paragraph (1) or (2).

## "Social Security" Taxes Paid By The Self-Employed

Theoretically, self-employed individuals acquire Social Security coverage by paying "Social Security" taxes in the form of a "self-employment" tax. This was not included in the original Act but was added in 1954. The forced inclusion of self-employed individuals into

Social Security exposes the whole phony "social" theory under which the program was promoted. People intelligent and disciplined enough to run their own business certainly don't need government bureaucrats (who do not have the ability and/or intelligence to do the same thing) to look after them. But, in any case, the so-called "self-employment Social Security tax" is another fraudulent Federal tax that no one is *required* to pay.

Figure 21 is Section 1401 of the Internal Revenue Code which theoretically established such a "Social Security" tax. Note again the deception employed by the headings, since nowhere does the "law" in either Sections (a) or (b) provide for "Old-age, survivors, and disability insurance" or "Hospital insurance". Both sections merely provide for a tax on "self-employment income" and *nothing more*! In Section (a)(5) the income tax for the period 12/31/81 — 1/1/85 is 8.05%; while in section (b)(4) the tax for the period 12/31/80 — 1/1/85 is 1.30% bringing the total tax to 9.8% for 1983. (The tax has now been increased to 11.3% for 1984).

## What Is "Self-Employment Income"?

Before "self-employment income" can be taxed, the government must tell us what it is. As explained earlier (see pages 31-35), the Code does not define "income" and, as expected, it doesn't define "self-employment income" either (though the Federal government very ingeniously seeks to create the illusion that it *is* defined). Since "self-employment income" is nowhere defined in the Code, the tax cannot exist and, on this basis alone, no one need pay such a "tax"!

### *The Government's Ping-Pong "Definition"*

Section 1402(b) of the Code (see Figure 22) states that ". . . the term 'self-employment income' means the net earnings from self-employment, derived by an indi-

# FIGURE 21

## CHAPTER 2.—TAX ON SELF-EMPLOYMENT INCOME

Sec.
1401. Rate of tax.
1402. Definitions.
1403. Miscellaneous provisions.

**Sec. 1401. Rate of tax.**

**(a) Old-age, survivors, and disability insurance.**

In addition to other taxes, there shall be imposed for each taxable year, on the self-employment income of every individual, a tax as follows:

(1) in the case of any taxable year beginning before January 1, 1978, the tax shall be equal to 7.0 percent of the amount of the self-employment income for such taxable year;

(2) in the case of any taxable year beginning after December 31, 1977, and before January 1, 1979, the tax shall be equal to 7.10 percent of the amount of the self-employment income for such taxable year;

(3) in the case of any taxable year beginning after December 31, 1978, and before January 1, 1981, the tax shall be equal to 7.05 percent of the amount of the self-employment income for such taxable year;

(4) in the case of any taxable year beginning after December 31, 1980, and before January 1, 1982, the tax shall be equal to 8.00 percent of the amount of the self-employment income for such taxable year;

(5) in the case of any taxable year beginning after December 31, 1981, and before January 1, 1985, the tax shall be equal to 8.05 percent of the amount of the self-employment income for such taxable year;

(6) in the case of any taxable year beginning after December 31, 1984, and before January 1, 1990, the tax shall be equal to 8.55 percent of the amount of the self-employment income for such taxable year; and

(7) in the case of any taxable year beginning after December 31, 1989, the tax shall be equal to 9.30 percent of the amount of the self-employment income for such taxable year.

FIGURE 21 (continued)

**(b) Hospital insurance.** ←

In addition to the tax imposed by the preceding subsection, there shall be imposed for each taxable year, on the self-employment income of every individual, a tax as follows:

(1) in the case of any taxable year beginning after December 31, 1973, and before January 1, 1978, the tax shall be equal to 0.90 percent of the amount of the self-employment income for such taxable year;

(2) in the case of any taxable year beginning after December 31, 1977, and before January 1, 1979, the tax shall be equal to 1.00 percent of the amount of the self-employment income for such taxable year;

(3) in the case of any taxable year beginning after December 31, 1978, and before January 1, 1981, the tax shall be equal to 1.05 percent of the amount of the self-employment income for such taxable year;

(4) in the case of any taxable year beginning after December 31, 1980, and before January 1, 1985, the tax shall be equal to 1.30 percent of the amount of the self-employment income for such taxable year;

(5) in the case of any taxable year beginning after December 31, 1984, and before January 1, 1986, the tax shall be equal to 1.35 percent of the amount of the self-employment income for such taxable year; and

(6) in the case of any taxable year beginning after December 31, 1985, the tax shall be equal to 1.45 percent of the amount of the self-employment income for such taxable year.

**(c) Relief from taxes in cases covered by certain international agreements.**

During any period in which there is in effect an agreement entered into pursuant to section 233 of the Social Security Act with any foreign country, the self-employment income of an individual shall be exempt from the taxes imposed by this section to the extent that such self-employment income is subject under such agreement to taxes or contributions for similar purposes under the social security system of such foreign country.

## FIGURE 22

### Code Sec. 1402

**(b) Self-employment income.**

The term "self-employment income" means the net earnings from self-employment derived by an individual (other than a nonresident alien individual) during any taxable year; except that such term shall not include—

vidual . . . during any taxable year. . .". So the "self-employment income tax" is, in reality, a "net earnings" tax. In other words, if "self-employment income" means "net earnings from self-employment" (and the tax is levied on "net earnings from self-employment"), then why isn't the tax called a "net earnings" tax instead of an "income" tax? The reason will be clear shortly, but it it apparent that we now have to find out the meaning of "net earnings" in order to know what is taxable as "self-employment income".

Figure 23 is Section 1402(a) of the code which presumably defines "net earnings from self-employment". We should be able to discover the meaning of "net earnings" from this Section; but, alas, we now find here that "net earnings" means "gross income" less allowable deductions — or, in other words, "net earnings" means "net income" and "net income" means "net earnings" and we are right back where we started!

What those rascals did was, in essence, to define a "big dog" as a "little horse" and a "little horse" as a "big dog". But they did it in such a confusing and complicated manner that no one understood what was going on. And who would squeal anyway — the lawyers and accountants who make money from the deception?

**FIGURE 23**

## Code Sec. 1402

**Sec. 1402. Definitions.**

**(a) Net earnings from self-employment.**

The term "net earnings from self-employment" means the gross income derived by an individual from any trade or business carried on by such individual, less the deductions allowed by this subtitle which are attributable to such trade or business, plus his distributive share (whether or not distributed) of income or loss described in section 702(a)(8) from any trade or business carried on by a partnership of which he is a member; except that in computing such gross income and deductions and such distributive share of partnership ordinary income or loss—

Proof that the IRS Code is a total fraud (and those who wrote it knew it!) can be deduced from this "ping-pong" definition between "net income" and "net earnings". Why were two definitions required? Why not one? The answer to this question reveals the whole illegal nature of Federal "income" taxes. The government could not constitutionally tax "earnings" since the 16th Amendment authorizes a tax on "income", not "earnings".[3] The tax therefore, had to be couched in terms of an "income" tax, (as explained on pages 87-88). But the Internal Revenue Code, as already explained, does not (and cannot) define "income" so the Federal government had to contrive a definition for "self-employment income" (employing the term "earnings" to do it) in the same manner it contrived a definition for

[3] But only if levied as an excise tax and not as a direct tax as is presently the case. See *Why No One Can Have Taxable Income* by Irwin Schiff.

"taxable income". So it proceeded to define "income" as "earnings" and then "earnings" as "income" (a distinction without a difference!) and the nation was none the wiser. At least we can admire the Federal Mafia's creativity! (Which is precisely what the Federal establishment *really* is. For proof see *The Schiff Report,* issues 1-6.)

### *"Can Self-Employment Income" Be Different From "Taxable Income"?*

Again, as I have already pointed out, the 16th Amendment only provides for a tax on "income" and not a tax on "self-employment" income (if different from "income" itself). So "self-employment income" legally has to mean the same thing as "taxable income" per Section 63 (Figure 10, page 34) or it is unconstitutional on its very face. The government, however, would have the public believe that it can *define* and *tax* "income" two different ways — one way under Section 63 and another way under Section 1401 — which it cannot legally do!

## Throw Him Into The Street If He Can't Pay His Social Security Tax

An attendee at an "untax seminar" I was conducting in Sioux Falls, South Dakota in 1977 told me the following story. It seems that he was a self-employed carpenter earning approximately $11,000 per year. However, since he had 9 or 10 children, he had enough deductions to eliminate any Federal "income" tax (even using the fictitious basis the IRS uses to calculate such taxes); and, as a result, he had not filed or paid Federal "income" taxes for a number of years. Somehow his case came to the attention of the IRS. He explained all this to them and they agreed that he had no Federal "income" taxes to pay. They said, however, that his "Social Security taxes" (i.e. self-employment taxes) were unrelated to his personal deductions or exemptions and, based upon his self-employment income over a number of years, he owed about $3,000 in unpaid Social Security taxes to the government.

Well, this individual told the IRS that he simply didn't have $3,000 to give them. As he explained to me, providing for so large a family took all the money he earned and he did not have a nickel left over with which to pay any portion of such a huge tax bill. So what did the IRS do? They put a lien on his house for the $3,000!!

He had come to my seminar extremely distraught and fearful since the IRS was threatening to auction off his house unless he paid the $3,000. He wanted to know if they *could* really throw him and his 9 children out into the street if he didn't pay up — as this was precisely what they were threatening to do! Apparently a benevolent government (one that installed Social Security as a means of "helping" people in their old age) was willing to take this couple's home away and throw them and their children out into the street in order to accomplish so noble a goal. How absurd can a situation be?

This poor man really didn't know what to do. He didn't have any extra money with which to pay the tax bill and he was petrified at the thought of being put out of his house with such a large family. He told me, "I don't know where else I can go!" I could offer him little *legal* help, since at that time I hadn't yet learned that all such IRS liens are illegal and that the Code does not provide for such a tax liablity.

I did suggest that he go to the local newspaper and tell them his story. I felt that the situation was so ludicrous that if he could just focus some publicity on the matter the IRS would probably back off. Apparently this approach worked. I was told that the story did appear in a Sioux Falls paper and the IRS did, indeed, back off. I wonder, though, how many others have had their homes seized and sold because they couldn't pay their "Social Security" taxes?

Over the years I have heard of at least two other cases where people have had liens put on their houses for allegedly failing to pay such "Social Security taxes". Should the government be in the position to take away a person's home in order to fund a project designed to "take care" of them in their old age?

But, apart from the obvious moral absurdity of the above, the Act's illegality should also be apparent. If this carpenter had no liablity for "income" taxes under Section 63, he couldn't have an "income" tax liability under any *other* section! Again, the 16th Amendment only provides for a tax on "income" and if citizens have no "income" that is taxable under Section 61 they can have no "income" (self-employment or otherwise) that is taxable under any other Code Section.

There is, of course, yet another reason why this "self-employment tax" is illegal. Presumably those who are self-employed have been made subject to two "income" taxes, while millions of other Americans — such as those who are retired and those who "work" for Federal and State governments — are only subject to one "income" tax. Again, such an assumption is legally ridiculous and totally repugnant to the Constitution. Therefore, all those who are self-employed can obviously stop paying their "self-employment *income* tax" on a variety of Constitutional grounds.

## How To Stop Paying "Self-Employment" Taxes

Self-employed individuals normally pay such "Social Security" taxes when they file quarterly tax estimates and when they file their final income tax returns. Since the law doesn't require anyone to file either a quarterly tax return or a final return,[4] dropping out of Social Security for the self-employeds is easy. They should just stop filing quarterly and annual tax returns altogether! Not only will they get out of "Social Security" and regular "income" taxes, but with all the time, money and aggravation they save, they will have more time and energy to devote to their businesses. Suddenly they will have the capital and time with which to expand. They will be able to hire more people. They will be able to turn out better products or deliver better and faster service. In short, self-employeds should stop paying these taxes so they'll be better able to serve their customers, their employees, their communities, their families and *their country*!

## SUMMARIZING THE POINTS COVERED IN CHAPTER 4

1. The portion of "Social Security" taxes paid by employers is a contrived "excise" tax on wages paid.
2. While the employers' tax (unlike the tax on employees) contains some elements of legitimacy, it, too, can be disregarded for the following reasons: 1) numerous provisions of the Social Security Act are obviously unconstitutional and thus render all taxes established under it null and void; 2) since Social Security taxes are admittedly not levied to "provide for the . . . general welfare of the United States", but levied to pay Social Security benefits, all such taxes are rendered unconstitutional on their very face; and 3) there is no provision in the law "requiring" employers to pay such taxes.
3. Since the law admits that the tax paid by em-

[4] This is explained in considerable detail in Irwin Schiff's *How Anyone Can Stop Paying Income Taxes.*

ployers is an "excise", the tax withheld from employees must be a direct tax. And since it is not apportioned it is openly and incontrovertibly unconstitutional.

4. There is nothing in the law itself that states that any portion of "Social Security" taxes paid by either employers or the self-employed goes for Social Security benefits.
5. "Social Security" taxes paid by the self-employed are levied in the guise of a "self-employment" tax, allegedly measured by "self-employment *income*".
6. The Code, however, does not define "self-employment income" and, therefore, such a tax cannot be legally extracted.
7. In any case, the 16th Amendment precludes the government from defining and taxing "self-employment income" on a different basis than "income" itself; and any attempt to do so is unconstitutional.
8. Self-employed individuals cannot be made subject to two "income" taxes while millions of retired Americans and government employees are made subject to only one.
9. Self-employed individuals can avoid paying "Social Security" taxes by no longer filing either quarterly tax estimates or final returns, in which case they will avoid paying regular "income" taxes along with "Social Security" taxes.
10. Self-employeds who stop paying "income" taxes will be in a much better position to expand their businesses, and thus will become far more valuable to their communities and to the nation.

# 5

# *The Supreme Court – Playing Games With The Law*

The Social Security Act covered a variety of new and far-reaching Federal programs and established a number of new taxes to go along with them. The Act's provisions were contained in eleven titles:

1. *Title I* created a new Federal charity program for the aged, based solely upon need.
2. *Title II* established a "Social Security" old-age retirement benefit for certain citizens based upon past wages.
3. *Title III* created a Federal scheme whereby people would now get paid for not working. This program was euphamistically called "unemployment insurance".
4. *Title IV* created a Federal charity program for "dependent" children.
5. *Title V* established another Federal charity program for "the health of mothers and children, especially in rural areas and in areas suffering from severe economic distress".
6. *Title VI* created a Federally financed service ". . . for the purpose of assisting states, counties . . . in establishing and maintaining public health services . . . ".

7. *Title VII* established a Social Security Board "... to make recommendation as to the most effective methods of providing economic security through social insurance ... " (which is a totally asinine concept and provides a fitting commentary on the Act as a whole).
8. *Title VIII* provided for "Social Security" taxes to be paid by certain employers and employees — though the government claimed these taxes were for *general* revenue purposes.
9. *Title IX* established a Federal tax on employers of eight or more (to fund unemployment "insurance") — though, again, the government claimed that such taxes were for *general* revenue purposes.
10. *Title X* established a Federally funded charity program specifically for the blind (why only for the blind?).
11. *Title XI* contained definitions and general provisions.

Figure 24 contains the first two sections of the original Title VIII. Note that the first paragraph of Title VIII is entitled "Income Tax on Employees" and confirms the fact that the so-called "Social Security" tax taken from employee paychecks is, in reality, just another "income" tax! The heading used in the original act showing this is far more accurate than the one used today (Figure 1, page 24). The original heading would still be in use today if it were not the government's intention to deliberately deceive the public as to what is really going on. The second paragraph (Section 802) also confirms that the tax is not a tax on wages but is merely "collected by the employer . . . *from* the wages as and when paid . . . "

## FIGURE 24

TITLE VIII—TAXES WITH RESPECT TO EMPLOYMENT

INCOME TAX ON EMPLOYEES !!

SECTION 801. In addition to other taxes, there shall be levied, collected, and paid upon the income of every individual a tax equal to the following percentages of the wages (as defined in section 811) received by him after December 31, 1936, with respect to employment (as defined in section 811) after such date:

(1) With respect to employment during the calendar years 1937, 1938, and 1939, the rate shall be 1 per centum.

(2) With respect to employment during the calendar years 1940, 1941, and 1942, the rate shall be 1½ per centum.

(3) With respect to employment during the calendar years 1943, 1944, and 1945, the rate shall be 2 per centum.

(4) With respect to employment during the calendar years 1946, 1947, and 1948, the rate shall be 2½ per centum.

(5) With respect to employment after December 31, 1948, the rate shall be 3 per centum.

DEDUCTION OF TAX FROM WAGES

SEC. 802. (a) The tax imposed by section 801 shall be collected by the employer of the taxpayer, by deducting the amount of the tax from the wages as and when paid. Every employer required so to deduct the tax is hereby made liable for the payment of such tax, and is hereby indemnified against the claims and demands of any person for the amount of any such payment made by such employer.

(b) If more or less than the correct amount of tax imposed by section 801 is paid with respect to any wage payment, then, under regulations made under this title, proper adjustments, with respect both to the tax and the amount to be deducted, shall be made, without interest, in connection with subsequent wage payments to the same individual by the same employer.

## Social Security Held to be Unconstitutional

On April 14, 1937, the Court of Appeals for the First Circuit in Boston, Massachusetts declared the Social Security Act unconstitutional on a variety of grounds. The opinion of that Court is contained in two excellently researched and written decisions[1] and came about when George P. Davis (a stockholder in both the Boston & Maine railroads and the Edison Electric Company of Boston) sought to enjoin each company from paying Social Security and unemployment compensation taxes on the grounds that such taxes were: 1) not authorized by the Constitution; 2) the Act infringed on the rights of the states; and 3) that the tax imposed ". . . a precarious and arbitrary burden on those who it affects". The Appellate Court agreed with Mr. Davis on all counts.

*Tax on Employers not a Lawful Excise Tax*

Citing numerous historical sources (Adam Smith's "The Wealth of Nations" and transcripts of State conventions related to the ratification of both Federal and State Constitutions) and case law, the Appellate Court correctly concluded that an excise tax as contemplated by the Constitution was a tax on articles of consumption and could not constitutionally apply to the mere employment of ordinary workers. As the court explained in *Davis vs. Boston* (page 374):

> In the discussions in the several state conventions, both as to the adoption of the Federal Constitution and with reference to the adoption of the respective state constitutions, it seems apparent that the understanding of the term "excise tax" was a tax laid upon articles of use or con-

[1] *Davis vs. Boston I.M.R. Co.* 89 F2nd 368 and *Davis vs. Edison Electric Illuminating Co. of Boston et al* 89 F2nd 393.

> sumption, not according to their value, but an arbitrary amount fixed by the Legislature; and the term "commodity" appears to have been used in its ordinary sense as including goods, wares, merchandise, produce of the land and manufacture.
>
> Massachusetts in framing its Constitution in 1780, in addition to the ordinary direct taxes, authorized the Legislature to impose "reasonable duties and excises upon any produce, goods, wares, merchandise and commodities whatsoever."

The Appellate Court also had ample Supreme Court case law to support its position. Here are but a few examples:

> "An inland imposition, paid sometimes upon the consumption of the commodity, or frequently upon the retail sale, which is the last stage before the consumption." And on page 618 of 184 U.S., 22 S.Ct. 493, 497, 46 L.Ed. 713: "To determine, then, what excise means, we have for our guidance, first, an enumeration of the articles that it fell on in Great Britain in 1787. We have, second, the nature of the tax as judicially determined; and we have, third, the definition of it, or the common understanding of men about it, as given by the Encyclopedia Brittanica and the Century Dictionary. Taking these three sources of information and combining them, it would seem that the leading idea of excise

> is that it is a tax, laid without rule or principle, upon consumable articles, upon the process of their manufacture and upon licenses to sell them." [2]

The Appellate Court went on to explain that the Supreme Court (in *Flint vs. Stone Tracy Co.* 220 U.S. 107) had held that:

> "Excises are 'taxes laid upon the manufacture, sale, or consumption of commodities within the country, upon licenses to pursue certain occupations, and upon corporate privileges,'"

Refusing to label a tax something that it obviously was not, the Court, again quoting from *Flint vs. Stone Tracy Co.*, stated:

> "While the mere declaration contained in a statute that it shall be regarded as a tax of a particular character does not make it such if it is apparent that it cannot be so designated consistently with the meaning and effect of the act," although such a declaration may "be entitled to some weight."

[2] *Davis vs. Boston*, p. 375, citing *Patton vs. Brady* 184 U.S. 608.

### *Tax Unconstitutionally Arbitrary*

In order to illustrate the arbitrary nature of the tax, the court used an example of an individual building his own house with day laborers. Such an individual, the Court pointed out, could " ... not be said to be engaged in the business of building houses or contracting ... " but would be doing " ... what every person has a natural right to do in the pursuit and in the exercise of liberty guaranteed him under the 5th Amendment of the Constitution ...".

> For instance, a physician or a lawyer may decide to construct a house for himself by day labor. In so doing he cannot be said to be engaged in the *business* of building houses or contracting; but simply doing what every person has a natural right to do in the pursuit of happiness and in the exercise of the liberty guaranteed to him under the Fifth Amendment of the Constitution. He employs common laborers, masons, carpenters, plumbers, electricians, painters, steamfitters, and it may well be that during the construction of his home he might find that he has had for one day, or a part of a day—though not at the same moment of time—during twenty weeks, though not even in consecutive weeks—eight employees at work in constructing his house; and, while it cannot be said that his business is that of house building, under section 907 of title IX (42 U.S.C.A. § 1107) he is subject to the tax imposed under section 901.

(pages 376–377)

With such examples the Court clearly exposed the illegal and arbitrary nature of the tax and also the government's absurd claim that the tax on employers was a legitimate excise. Citing additional case law to support these arguments, the Court stated that an individual who ". . . enjoyed no franchise or special privilege by the legislature but was exercising a common right could not be made subject to an excise tax . . .". Developing this argument further the court said:

> "The right to set up and maintain theatres and other places of public amusement is not natural and inherent. Working by an artisan at his trade, carrying on an ordinary business, or engaging in a common occupation or calling cannot be subjected to a license fee or excise. These plainly are not affected with a public interest" [3]
>
> (page 376)

> "The rights to labor and to do ordinary business are natural, essential and inalienable, partaking of the nature both of personal liberty and of private property."
>
> (page 376)

[3] Citing *Gleason vs. McKay* 134 Mass 419 and *O'Keefe vs. Somrville* 190 Mass 110.

> But nowhere do we find that an excise tax has ever been imposed in this country on the natural right to employ labor in manufacturing, or in any trade or calling for profit.
>
> (page 376)

> It is urged that the tax imposed under section 901 of title IX (42 U.S.C.A. § 1101) is imposed on the privilege of doing business. If Congress had so intended, we think it would have said so. Section 901 does not impose a tax on any business in which any employer may be engaged, nor on the manufacture of any goods, wares, merchandise, or commodity, but solely with respect to having in one's employ eight or more employees, the amount of the tax being based on the amount of the total pay roll.
>
> (page 376)

### *Tax Unconstitutional — Not for the "General Welfare"*

Another reason the Court found the Act unconstitutional is that it violated the general welfare clause of the Constitution. The Court noted that the taxes to be collected were to be used for the specific benefit of some and not for others and, therefore, the tax was not for the "general welfare of the United States" as provided by Article 1, Section 8, Paragraph 1 of the Constitution.[4] On this issue the Court stated:

> "A tax, in the general understanding of the term, and as used in the Constitution, signifies an exaction for the support of the government. The word has never been thought to connote the expropriation of money from one group for the benefit of another. * * * The exaction cannot be wrested out of its setting, denominated an excise for raising revenue and legalized by ignoring its purpose as a mere instrumentality for bringing about a desired end. To do this would be to shut our eyes to what all others than we can see and understand."

and . . .

> If the act is carried out as planned by Congress, and a tax is imposed on every employer which is credited against a tax

[4] According to Article 1, Section 8, paragraph 1, the Federal government is only authorized to collect taxes for the "general welfare of the United States" and not for the specific welfare of some groups to the exclusion of others. Of course, the government today now violates this provision with total impunity and does not feel bound by it in any manner, shape or form, thanks in large measure to its success in getting Social Security through the courts.

> imposed by the state, and, under the conditions imposed by section 302 and 303 of title III and section 903 of title IX (42 U.S.C.A. §§ 502, 503, 1103), is paid to employees found to be eligible, it amounts, in effect, to taking the property of every employer for the benefit of a certain class of employees. The entire plan, viewed as a whole, is an attempt to do indirectly what Congress cannot do directly, and to assume national control over a subject clearly within the jurisdiction of the states.

> [9] Therefore, to provide unemployment benefits regardless of need, to persons who have worked in local employments in local trade and manufacturing within a state, not related to interstate commerce, or in any calling not related to the matters subject to the control of the Congress, is not to provide for the general welfare of the United States.

It is important to note that the Appellate Court looked at the entire Social Security Act (all eleven titles) as a whole. The Federal government, on the other hand, in arguing the Act's constitutionality, had the nerve to contend that *the revenue sections of the Act were not in any way connected to the benefit sections!* If that truth were admitted, the open and shut unconstitutionality of the Act would have been uncontested! But an honorable Appellate Court was not going to buy the government's absurd claim that the Act's taxes and related benefits were separate and not tied together. The Court stated it was not going to "shut (its) eyes to what all others . . . can see and understand . . .". Convinced beyond any doubt that the entire Social Security Act was unconstitutional, the Court declared it so and included in its opinion the following stirring passage taken from yet another[5] Supreme Court decision:

> " 'The Constitution, in all its provisions, looks to an indestructible Union, composed of indestructible States.' Every journey to a forbidden end begins with the first step; and the danger of such a step by the federal government in the direction of taking over the powers of the states is that the end of the journey may find the states so despoiled of their powers, or—what may amount to the same thing—so relieved of the responsibilities which possession of the powers necessarily enjoins, as *to reduce them to little more than geographical subdivisions of the national domain.* It is safe to say that if, when the Constitution was under consideration, it had been thought that any such danger lurked behind its plain words, it would never have been ratified."

*Davis vs. Boston,* page 377)

[5] *Davis vs. Boston,* page 377, citing *Carter vs. Carter Coal Co.* 298 U.S. 238.

Then these learned judges added these prophetic passages:

> That this amounts to coercion of the states and control by Congress of a matter clearly within the province of the states cannot be denied. If valid, it marks the end of responsible state government in any field in which the United States chooses to take control by the use of its taxing power. If the United States can take control of unemployment insurance and old age assistance by the coercive use of taxation, it can equally take control of education and local health conditions by levying a heavy tax and remitting it in the states which conform their educational system or their health laws to the dictates of a federal board.
>
> It is plainly the duty of the courts to uphold and support the present Constitution until it has been changed in the legal way.

(page 377)

and . . .

> In this sense, Congress has not an unlimited power of taxation; but it is limited to specific objects,—the payment of the public debts, and providing for the common defense and general welfare. A tax, therefore, laid by

Congress for neither of these objects, would be unconstitutional, as an excess of its legislative authority."

(page 375)

## Supreme Court Arbitrarily Reverses Lower Court's Decision

On May 24, 1937 (a day that should live in infamy) a perfidious Supreme Court reversed the Appellate Court's sound decisions and held the Social Security Act constitutional.[6] On that day the Court arbitrarily and illegally affected a fundamental change in America's political, economic and social structure (which has cost the nation dearly ever since) and clearly demonstrated that the Court's lack of economic understanding was at least matched by its obvious ignorance of the Constitution or its willingness to subvert it.[7]

In arguing Social Security's unconstitutionality before the Supreme Court, Davis raised only two issues:

1. That the Act sought to raise revenue "for a particular purpose, not merely to produce revenue for the United States"; and that
2. the imposition of the tax on employers was not

[6] In *Helvering vs. Davis* 301 U.S.C. 619 and *Steward Machine Co. vs. Davis* 301 U.S. 548 (both decided on the same day) the Court (in Steward) did not address the First Circuit decision directly but affirmed a Fifth Circuit decision which had upheld as Constitutional the unemployment tax imposed by Title IX. Both cases, however, involved the same issues and the Court did note the First Circuit's contrary holding in its decision.

[7] Two Supreme Court Justices, McReynolds and Butler, agreed with the lower court and stated their belief that the Act was repugnant to the 10th Amendment of the Constitution.

an excise tax within the meaning of the Constitution.[8]

It is important to note that since these were the only issues raised in this case, these were the only issues that the Supreme Court needed to address. As you will discover, the Act is blatantly unconstitutional on a variety of other grounds — none of which were raised in this or any other case.

## Employers are "Agents" and "Stakeholders"

The government first attempted to knock out Davis's case by claiming that Davis himself had no standing to even challenge the Act's constitutionality. The government contended that he was acting merely as a stockholder and not as the actual payer of any of the taxes imposed by the Act. In pursuing this argument, the government made a number of interesting observations. It argued that ". . . since the employer is merely a *withholding agent* with respect to the employee tax, neither corporation or stockholder may ask for relief from it . . ."; and that ". . . the employee tax is a withholding at the source, the employer being a *collecting agent* or *stakeholder*. The withholding provisions themselves *are not challenged* nor could they be successfully attacked . . .". (emphasis added in both quotes)

Since Davis had not even raised (much less *attacked*) the withholding provision, one wonders why the government even brought it up. But the government's claim that such provisions could not be "successfully attacked" is ridiculous since the withholding provision, *if mandatory, would be unconstitutional on its very face!*

First of all, the government admits that the em-

[8] All references refer to *Helvering vs. Davis,* supra.

ployer is made an "agent" of the government. Where in the Constitution is the Federal government empowered to *force* private citizens to be its agents? In addition, a "stakeholder", as defined in *Black's Law Dictionary,* is ". . . a person with whom money is deposited pending the decision of a debt or wager . . . a third person chosen by two or more persons to keep in deposit property, the right or possession of which is contested between them, and to be delivered to the one who shall establish his right to it".

Can private employers, therefore, be made government "stakeholders" without first *agreeing* to accept the job? Did employees *agree* to have their employers act as their stakeholders? And, if employers are, in fact, "stakeholders", how can they deliver the funds they hold to the government before the government "shall establish (its) right to it . . . "?

## *Violation of the 13th Amendment*

Nowhere in the Constitution is the Federal government empowered to force private citizens into government service as unpaid agents and/or stakeholders. As a matter of fact, the Constitution expressly prohibits it! Working for the Federal government as its *agent* (without pay) is "involuntary servitude" and is specifically barred by the 13th Amendment. However, the withholding "law" need not be challenged on this ground since the "law", remember, doesn't *require* (see page 44) anyone to withhold such taxes — employers are simply tricked and intimidated into doing it. The law contains no such requirement because, if it did, the law would be unconstitutional for the reason just described. Therefore, any employer who does not want to continue being the government's unpaid "agent" or "stakeholder" can immediately stop withholding Social Security taxes from employee wages.

## Social Security Taxes Not "Earmarked"

How did the government respond to Davis's claim that Social Security taxes were unconstitutional because they were earmarked for specific purposes? The government claimed that they *were not earmarked!* Social Security taxes, the government argued, were ". . . true taxes, the purpose being simply to raise revenue. No compliance with any scheme or Federal regulation is involved. The proceeds are paid, unrestricted, into the Treasury as Internal Revenue collections, available for the general support of government; that the appropriations were wholly independent appropriations . . . "; and, thus, the Court could not deprive the revenue so raised of the "quality as a true taxing measure".

Thus, arguing before the Supreme Court, the government claimed that Social Security taxes were not earmarked for any purpose whatsoever. Is that what the government has been telling the American public? If Social Security taxes go into the Treasury as "ordinary tax collections" (to be used for whatever purposes the government chooses), what were the so-called "trust funds" all about? If Social Security collections are paid "unrestricted into the Treasury", how do we account for those headings shown in Figures 1 and 2. *If the government had taken the position suggested by those section headings, the Supreme Court would have had no choice but to declare the Act unconstitutional!* So, in order to get Social Security through the courts, the government had to argue a position exactly opposite from what it has been telling the public! The government's hypocracy on this matter was so obvious that an honest Appellate Court wouldn't buy it. A hypocritical Supreme Court, on the other hand, was able to deal with it in a very inventive manner (as you will see)!

## Government's Main Argument

What was the government's main argument to the court? The government claimed:

> The expenditures in the present case are clearly well within the limits of the power of Congress. The number of aged persons in this country is rapidly increasing; workers in urban industrialized civilization usually arrive at old age without adequate means for self-support, as is demonstrated not only by their earning powers during their working lifetime but by various studies which have been made of the extent of dependency of people over 65 years of age. Those who are able to call upon their children for support only aggravate the evil by depriving the younger members of the family of the resources which they need. Voluntary industrial pension plans cover but a few. Private charity is inadequate to cope with the problem. Even state old age benefit laws present grave administrative and financial problems.
>
> Therefore, the expenditures contemplated by Title II are for the general welfare of the United States. Moreover, the form of the expenditures is soundly designed to promote general welfare. The statute excludes employed aged persons, thereby providing a simple and easily administered means test which is legally sufficient. *Mountain Timber Co.* v. *Washington*, 243 U. S. 219, 230. The payments themselves are graduated both by wages and length of employment, so as to provide an incentive to work and at the same time roughly to relate benefits to past standards of living.

The Act does not require retirement from employment and has no tendency to induce it. It does not constitute a plan for compulsory insurance within the accepted meaning of the term "insurance."

Thus the government's main argument for Social Security was a contrived and absurd socio-economic one. If American workers in 1936 arrived at "old age without adequate means of self-support", the obvious question was why? Why should 20th Century Americans have been more dependent in their old age than 18th Century Americans? Hadn't America made any economic progress in 150 years?

If a majority of Americans could arrive at old age being more dependent — and if their lives had become economically more hazardous than Americans living 150 years before — then America had obviously not made any economic progress since the Constitution was adopted. A nation makes such progress when it becomes progressively easier for all segments of society to exist. The disparity between economic classes might widen, but given improvements in technology and increases in capital formation, living at all social levels must become progressively easier if economic progress is being made. If empirical evidence shows that the reverse is happening, then an investigation is obviously called for to explain how such an anomoly can occur! The problem (if, indeed, it existed) cannot be summarily solved by merely passing laws! If it were that simple, then politicians could presumably pass laws to solve all of society's economic and social problems!

*Taking Care of One's Parents*

Notice the government's attempt to equate the discharge of an obvious filial responsibility (taking care of one's parents) into some kind of social and economic "evil". Also, if it is society's responsibility to take care of the elderly, what will motivate individuals to make provisions to take care of this contingency on their own? And if children are not responsible for the support of their *own* parents, who *is* responsible? Strangers?

Implicit in the government's whole argument is the assumption that taking care of individuals is a legitimate, constitutional concern of the Federal government (which it is not) and, further, that the Federal government possesses unlimited, independent wealth with which to pursue such an objective. Obviously the government intended (because of this program) to increase taxes which, in itself, would deprive "the younger members of the family of . . . resources . . . they need". So, younger members of society were going to be financially deprived one way or another! And, if private employers choose not to install pensions, does the Constitution then empower the Federal government to *force* them to do so?

## Court: Federal Power Not Limited by the Constitution

Pensions, remember, are an indirect labor cost and must be born (like wages) out of labor's productivity. Money paid into pensions cannot be used for salaries, so can the government legally force employers to pay lower wages (as they now do) in order to install government favored pensions? Does the Constitution allow the Federal government to force such choices on private business or to take over any economic function it desires simply by alleging that private capital or state governments are "inadequate" for the job? If functions which lie wholly within the constitutional authority of state government become "administrative and financial problems", does the Constitution then give the Federal government the power to replace them? If the answers to these questions are "yes", then the powers of the Federal government *are not* limited by the Constitution at all!

*Government Admits "Insurance" Claim A Lie*

Note further the government's contention *to the Court* that Social Security taxes are not "insurance" but *to the public* they have incessantly (and reduntantly) claimed otherwise. (see pages 209-215).

Note, also, the government's claim that a program that admittedly only pays "benefits if you stop work" will have "no tendency" to induce "not working". Such a claim was, of course, pure unadulterated poppycock and the government knew it. Every reader knows of individuals who stopped working simply because they became eligible for Social Security benefits. But the government absurdly claimed and argued otherwise in order to get Social Security through the courts.

## How Did the Supreme Court Respond?

Since (as you will see) the Court obviously wanted to hold the Act constitutional, it contrived arguments to enable it to do so. First of all, Justice Cordoza (writing for the court) stated:

> In this case Titles VIII and II are the subject of attack. Title VIII lays another excise upon employ-

> ers in addition to the one imposed by Title IX (though with different exemptions). It lays a special income tax upon employees to be deducted from their wages and paid by the employers. Title II provides for the payment of Old Age Benefits, and supplies the motive and occasion, in the view of the assailants of the statute, for the levy of the taxes imposed by Title VIII. The plan of the two titles will now be summarized more fully.
>
> Title VIII, as we have said, lays two different types of tax, an "income tax on employees," and "an excise tax on employers." The income tax on employees is measured by wages paid during the calendar year. § 801. The excise tax on the employer is to be paid "with respect to having individuals in his employ," and, like the tax on employees, is measured by wages. § 804. Neither tax is applicable to certain types of employment, such as agricultural labor, domestic service, service for the national or state governments, and service performed by persons who have attained the age of 65 years. § 811
>
> (emphasis added)

This passage shows that despite Cordoza's vaunted reputation the Justice had no real understanding of:

1. The taxing clauses of the United States Constitution;
2. the Social Security law that he was attempting to judge; and
3. the equal protection clause of the United States Constitution.

If Cordoza understood the taxing clauses of the Constitution and the 16th Amendment he would have realized that the Federal government could not possibly lay "a *special* income tax on employees". Either the tax was an *income* tax or it was not. The 16th

Amendment makes no provision for "a *special* income tax". But if the law imposed a *new* "income" tax, it obviously had to apply to *all* Americans who had "income", not just to some, and so the Act could not exclude from such a tax the "income" received by agricultural workers, domestic employees, state and Federal employees, employees of non-profit corporations, and, of course, those who were self-employed and retired. How could Cordoza not have known that the Federal government could not possibly levy an "income" tax on one segment of society while excluding numerous others from the same "income" tax?!

Note, also, Cordoza's statement that the "income tax on employees is measured by wages during the calendar year". This statement is complete nonsense! If it were true, the "income" tax would not be a tax on "income" but a tax on *wages*! A tax on *income* obviously has to be measured by "income" not *wages*. The "income" tax was to be *deducted* from wages (based on a *percentage* of those wages) and it obviously cannot be "measured by wages", but *must be measured by income.*

If the tax on employees was to be "measured by wages", why didn't the act specifically say so? It could easily have said, ". . . in addition to other taxes there shall be levied upon the wages of every individual a tax equal to the following percentage of wages." The reason that the act was not worded in this way is that such wording would have immediately rendered the Act unconstitutional! Such wording would have cleary established the tax as an unapportioned *direct* tax on property (wages) and such a tax was held to be unconstitutional by the Supreme Court in 1895.[9] The Supreme

[9] *Pollack vs. Farmers Loan & Trust Co.* 158 U.S. 429.

Court ruled later[10] (in 1915, subsequent to the passage of the 16th Amendment) that the 16th Amendment allowed the government to levy an *excise* (indirect) tax on "income" as long as the tax on income was "separated from the source" of that income. Thus, in 1935 a direct tax on "income" (without apportionment) was *theoretically* possible while a direct tax on wages (without apportionment) was not. (Because the "direct" tax on *income* had to be levied in the form of an "excise" tax—actually making it an "indirect" tax in the Constitutional sense. These important Constitutional distinctions will be clarified in my next book.) So the government very sneakily worded the Act so as to be a direct tax on "income" in order to get within the law; but then proceeded to enforce the "law" as if it were a direct tax on "wages" which it was not! Worse yet, the Supreme Court allowed them to get away with it! *Such is the type of legislative treachery that is practiced by the Federal government with the help of our "courts".*

## Social Security Taxes Admittedly Unconstitutional

When Cordoza stated that Title VIII laid *two different* types of taxes ("an excise tax on employers" and "a special income tax on employees") he openly admitted that the new "income" tax on employees (admittedly not an excise tax) was obviously a *direct* tax. And, since the Court has openly admitted that the tax on employees is a direct tax (since it's *not* an excise tax), it has to be apportioned according to Article 1, Section 2, Paragraph 3 and Article 1, Section 9, paragraph 4 of the

[10] *Brushaber vs. Pacific RR* 240 U.S. 1.

Constitution.[11] Since it is not being apportioned, it is *(by Cordoza's own admission)* openly unconstitutional! Cordoza's admission provides all the proof that is needed that the entire Social Security Act is unconstitutional on at least two grounds, both of which are irrefutible since they have already been admitted by the Supreme Court:

1. The tax withheld from employee wages is an unapportioned direct tax; and
2. numerous Americans having "income" were specifically excluded from paying the tax in obvious violation of the taxing and equal protection clauses of the Constitution.

### *Employees Didn't Complain (Hah!)*

The government also argued that "no employee is complaining". Obviously no employee at that time had the knowledge, time or money to challenge the Act. If any employee today challenges the Act on either of the above two grounds, the Act must fall on *these two issues alone*. But no employee need waste his money or time in court challenging the constitutionality of this "income" tax. The Court's admission provides all the necessary proof that the tax (if mandatory) is unconstitutional and all employers and employees are, therefore, free to disregard it. I, of course, will continue with my analysis in order to enlarge this exposé of both the tax and the Federal judiciary.

[11] The 16th Amendment *did not* amend or change these apportionment provisions *in any way*. All the 16th Amendment did was to remove a tax on "income" from these sections and place it into Article 1, Section 8, paragraph 1, clause 2. See *Brushaber vs. Pacific RR* 240 U.S. 1.

## Court's Decision Based on Economic Misconceptions, Not Law

What reasoning did the Supreme Court employ to justify the tax? The Court basically accepted the government's sophomoric socio-economic theories. That the Court's decision was not based upon law but upon such socio-economic misconceptions is obvious from the following passage:

> The purge of nation-wide calamity that began in 1929 has taught us many lessons. Not the least is the solidarity of interests that may once have seemed to be divided. Unemployment spreads from State to State, the hinterland now settled that in pioneer days gave an avenue of escape. *Home Building & Loan Assn.* v. *Blaisdell,* 290 U. S. 398, 442. Spreading from State to State, unemployment is an ill not particular but general, which may be checked, if Congress so determines, by the resources of the Nation. If this can have been doubtful until now, our ruling today in the case of the *Steward Machine Co., supra,* has set the doubt at rest. But the ill is all one, or at least not greatly different, whether men are thrown out of work because there is no longer work to do or because the disabilities of age make them incapable of doing it. Rescue becomes necessary irrespective of the cause. The hope behind this statute is to save men and women from the rigors of the poor house as well as from the haunting fear that such a lot awaits them when journey's end is near.
>
> Congress did not improvise a judgment when it found that the award of old age benefits would be conducive to the general welfare.

(emphasis added)

The utter hypocracy of this reasoning became obvious when the government expanded Social Security to include the self-employed. Those capable of operating their own businesses are certainly capable enough to see to their own old age and disability needs. And, if they aren't, are the bureaucrats employed by the Federal government *more capable*?!

### *A Nation of Men, Not Laws*

In addition, the Court argued that "the concept of the general welfare (is not) static. Needs that were narrow or parochial a century ago may be interwoven in our day with the well-being of the nation. What is critical or urgent changes with the times".

Here the court apparently argues that the Federal government can take whatever power it wants depending on the "times". Have we, therefore, become a nation not of laws but of men who can bend the law based upon *their reading* of "the times"? Of course the Court is wrong on this count, too. The Federal government was given *specific and limited powers* within the Constitution and it has no authority to increase that power because of "changing times" (except perhaps, during wartime emergency). As far as Cordoza and Justices of his philosophy are concerned, the government is apparently at liberty to twist the Constitution to fit whatever political expediency strikes its fancy.

### *Private Property can be Taken for Political Purposes*

One of Cordoza's observations was that unemployment can be checked "by the resources of the nation". What resources does "the nation" possess that are available to check unemployment? Do private resources automatically become public resources which the government is free to confiscate in an idiotic, politically inspired attempt to end "unemployment"? How about Cordoza's argument that unemployment can develop because "there is no longer work to do or because the disabilities of age make them incapable of doing it"? There is always work "to do" since human wants and desires are limitless. But the real and underlying causes of unemployment obviously escape Cordoza's limited economic understanding.

### *Economic Problems Always Aggravated By Government*

It is the idiotic and destructive nature of government's economic and fiscal legislation that causes economic breakdowns and unemployment to occur.[12] Otherwise society (barring natural disasters) would experience continuous improvement in its standard of living.[13] So all of Cordoza's social and economic concerns were created by government, and he and the other Justices were further deluded by the belief that even *more* government could solve them! Why don't Supreme Court Justices stick to simply trying to figure out the applicable law without involving themselves in economic issues for which they have no particular training or expertise? Since when is constitutional law based on economics anyway?

### *Can the Government Support the People?*

Note further Cordoza's pathetically naive statement that "the hope behind the statute is to save men

[12] The high level of juvenile and minority unemployment is directly attributable to the Federal minimum wage law, see *The Biggest Con,* pages 164–184.

[13] See *The Biggest Con,* pages 264–289. (Schiff; Hamden, CT: Freedom Books, 1977.)

and women from the rigors of the poor house as well as from the haunting fear that such a lot awaits them when journey's end is near".

Even overlooking the naiveté of this statement, where *in the Constitution* is the Federal government empowered to attempt to "save men and women from the rigors of the poor house"?[14] And what assets can the government lawfully draw on to do it? In reality it is government that is now driving men and women to the poor house because of all the wealth it takes from them in the guise of legitimate taxation! Obviously this passage demonstrates the Court's Pollyanna belief that government can support the people, when men of intelligence should understand that it is the other way around!

This statement also demonstrates how far this nation has travelled since 1897 when Grover Cleveland vetoed an act of Congress designed to aid some Texas counties affected by drought by stating, "I can find no warrant for such an appropriation in the Constitution. The lesson should be constantly enforced that though the people should support the government, the government should not support the people".

With this decision the Supreme Court (among other things) revealed that it was totally oblivious to a fundamental constitutional concept that Cleveland had expressed so well.

[14] A socialist government is free to adopt such objectives (it adopts but never delivers them); but are such objectives compatible with the powers granted to the Federal government in the U.S. Constitution and the powers and rights reserved by it to the states and to the people themselves?

## The Court's Duplicity Irrefutable

If you harbor any illusions that the Supreme Court is an honorable institution that seeks to uphold, protect, and defend the United States Constitution, prepare to shed them now. In this case the Supreme Court actually refused to face one of the only two legal issues brought before it (see page 78). Overlooking completely the Court's feeble and contrived effort to refute the lower court's finding that the tax on employers was not a valid excise, look at how the Court handled the other issue — namely that since the tax and benefit sections of the Act were intertwined, the taxes were unconstitutional since they were not "for the general welfare of the United States" as required by the Constitution. Since the "Court's" action on this issue is so outrageous, I've reproduced the entire page (Figure 25) so you can see the Court's actual words with your own eyes.

Note that the Court states "the argument for the respondent (Davis) is that the provisions of the two titles dovetail in such a way as to justify the conclusion that Congress would have been unwilling to pass one without the other." (OBVIOUSLY!) "The argument for the petitioners (the government) is that the tax moneys are not earmarked and that Congress is at liberty to spend them as it will. The usual separality clause is embodied in the act . . . " Well, this is what this case was about, all right. Let's see how the Court decided the issue. Incredulously, look what the Court said: "We find it unnecessary to make a choice between the arguments and so leave the question open." CAN YOU BELIEVE IT!? Leave the question open? Why? This was the most important of the two issues that Davis raised, so why didn't the Court rule on the matter? It was because they obviously could not address this without declaring the Social Security Act unconstitutional! So those black-

## FIGURE 25



may sap those sturdy virtues and breed a race of weaklings. If Massachusetts so believes and shapes her laws in that conviction, must her breed of sons be changed, he asks, because some other philosophy of government finds favor in the halls of Congress? But the answer is not doubtful. One might ask with equal reason whether the system of protective tariffs is to be set aside at will in one state or another whenever local policy prefers the rule of *laissez faire.* The issue is a closed one. It was fought out long ago.[10] When money is spent to promote the general welfare, the concept of welfare or the opposite is shaped by Congress, not the states. So the concept be not arbitrary, the locality must yield. Constitution, Art. VI, Par. 2.

*Third.* Title II being valid, there is no occasion to inquire whether Title VIII would have to fall if Title II were set at naught.

The argument for the respondent is that the provisions of the two titles dovetail in such a way as to justify the conclusion that Congress would have been unwilling to pass one without the other. The argument for petitioners is that the tax moneys are not earmarked, and that Congress is at liberty to spend them as it will. The usual separability clause is embodied in the act. § 1103.

We find it unnecessary to make a choice between the arguments, and so leave the question open.

*Fourth.* The tax upon employers is a valid excise or duty upon the relation of employment.

As to this we need not add to our opinion in *Steward Machine Co.* v. *Davis, supra,* where we considered a like question in respect of Title IX.

---

[10] IV Channing, History of the United States, p. 404 (South Carolina Nullification); 8 Adams, History of the United States (New England Nullification and the Hartford Convention).

robed scoundrels ducked the issue entirely by saying that they would "leave the question open". Why should the question of the constitutionality of a law which would drastically change the entire social, economic and political landscape of the nation be left "open"? "Open" for what? "Open" for when? So someone else could make the long, legal trek *back* to the Supreme Court to have a question decided that had already been before it?

But if a cowardly and deceitful Supreme Court refused to address this question, an honest Court of Appeals did and found Social Security unconstitutional *on this very issue!* Even though the Supreme Court refused to rule on this important issue, why shouldn't it have been settled on the basis of the Appellate Court's finding that this issue rendered the Act unconstitutional? And, more importantly, if the Supreme Court did leave this question "open" in its 1937 decision, the issue has since been conclusively settled by the government itself.

The government now openly admits (pages 169-170) that Social Security taxes are needed to pay Social Security benefits. Indeed, Social Security taxes are now routinely increased (admittedly) for no other purpose than to pay mounting Social Security costs. So does the government now dare contend that such tax increases "are not earmarked" and that their purpose is "just to raise revenue" for the government?

It is clear that the Supreme Court upheld Social Security's constitutionality not on the basis of law (which it *refused* to face) but, rather, on the basis of its own economic and social (never mind legal) misconceptions. What is equally depressing is the realization that today's Supreme Court is no better than the pathetic panel that found this piece of socialistic tripe (repugnant in every way to the U.S. Constitution) to be constitutional.

## SUMMARIZING THE POINTS COVERED IN CHAPTER 5

1. An honest Appellate Court found Social Security unconstitutional on a variety of grounds.
2. A dishonest Supreme Court didn't!!

# 6

# How Social Security Was Sold To The Public - Would They Buy It Today?

The Federal government sold Social Security to the nation on a basis that is entirely different from how it operates that program today. Further, there is no question that if the politicians in 1935 proposed Social Security in its current form, they would have been laughed right out of office. In addition, it is equally clear that even a biased Supreme Court could never have held today's Social Security program constitutional.

## An "Insurance" Program

Social Security was sold to the American public as an "insurance" program. The politicians simply took advantage of the public's faith and trust in America's respected life insurance industry (which, unlike the banks, had just come through the depression without causing any losses to the public) to sell their socialist scam to them. The government claimed Social Security was going to have gigantic "insurance reserves." These "reserves" would be created from the "contributions" of employees and employers from which future benefits would be paid. The nation was told that these huge reserves would reach their "full fruition" by 1980 when they would, with only modest tax supplements, be capable of carrying the program along into the indefinite future. And the public swallowed it!

### *Gigantic Reserves Contemplated*

Look, for example, at this excerpt from a *New York Times* editorial of December 15, 1935 in which the proposed Social Security program was discussed:

> "The plan contemplates the building up of the most *gigantic reserve,* estimated to reach over $50,000,000,000 by 1980. The freezing of so much sorely needed purchasing power cannot but hamper recovery.[1] The problem of investing such *huge sums* will prove insuperable. No one can guarantee that such *fantastic governmental credits* will ever be made good.[2] *Large reserves* are always in danger of being usurped by politicians for other purposes,[3] as experiences with other funds amply testifies. Should even a partial inflation wipe out some of these funds;[4] no one can calculate the menace it will create. (emphasis added).

*The New York Times* was (correctly) skeptical of these "reserves". "The problem of investing such funds", the *Times* observed, "will prove insuperable." Well, it really proved to be no problem at all since the government never invested one dime of it! (see page 217).

[1], [2],[3],[4] The writer of this editorial clearly foresaw the numerous inherent dangers in the Social Security concept. And the government, as feared, delivered every one of them!

Note, however, the size of the "reserve" that the government was projecting (and the nation was seriously contemplating) — $50 BILLION by 1980! Actually by 1980 the fictitious Social Security reserve (for the programs) was reported at $22.8 billion — but $50 billion in 1935 was a whole lot different than $50 billion in 1980. So let us put that $50 billion "reserve" into its proper 1935 perspective.

The total Federal revenue in 1935 was $3.3 billion (the government now spends that in a day-and-a-half) so this projected "reserve" amounted to 15 years of Federal receipts! By contrast, the actual reported 1980 "reserve" amounted to federal expenditures for 12 days![5]

This will give you some idea of the magnitude of the "reserve" that the nation foresaw. The public also believed that these "reserves" would be real and not imaginary! Can you see how financially formidable Social Security was made to appear? But the above "reserve" picture tells only half the story. Remember, these projected "reserves" were only expected to finance *modest* Social Security benefits (as compared to what Social Security promises today).

The projected $50 billion "reserve" was not expected to "insure" 1) substantial survivors' benefits (a feature that was not added until 1939 and then greatly expanded over the years); 2) disability benefits (not added until 1956); 3) Medicare (added in 1965); nor 4)

[5] By October, 1982, the OASI (Old Age and Survivors Insurance) "reserve" was *totally exhausted* and OASI checks were sent out on the basis of the government "borrowing" from the other two "funds" — the Disability and Hospital "funds". These accounts reportedly had "reserves" of $27.7 billion at year's end, while the OASI account was now *minus* $2.6 billion.

the millions of people subsequently brought into the plan who were initially excluded. In addition, the maximum projected retirement benefit in 1980 was $572.00 as opposed to the $85.00 maximum projected retirement benefit in 1935. It is safe to say that the total Social Security package by 1980 was at least 20 times greater than what was contemplated by the *Times* editorial writer.[6] To him the "gigantic reserve" must have appeared to be the equivalent of at least $20 trillion when viewed in today's terms. No wonder he was skeptical!

*Not Like The Townsend Plan*

As I mentioned previously, while Social Security was being debated, Dr. Francis E. Townsend was beating a loud drum for his own proposed retirement program; and millions of Americans (uninformed ones to be sure) were taking his plan seriously. His program called for paying everyone over sixty $200 per month (if they agreed to spend it in 30 days!) to be financed by a national sales tax. To be sure, Townsend's activities did generate a certain amount of political and social pressure.

*The New York Times* of December 15, 1935 even devoted an entire editorial to Townsend captioned, "TOWNSEND'S SOLDIERS", and commented that ". . .

[6] The maximum combined tax on employees had increased from $60 in 1937 to $3,175 in 1980, or better than 50 times. Combined payments in 1984 will be $5,178 or 86 times greater and are projected to reach $8,722 by 1990. In the past, though, all such government projections have proved to be optimistically low! Also, the cost per family can even be greater than these figures if both husband and wife work since there are no income limitations on employer payments.

last week Dr. Townsend decided that his followers should name candidates for President and Vice President in every state . . .". As you can see, Townsend was getting considerable national attention. As a matter of fact, the December 20th issue carried a front page story of a debate which took place between news columnist George E. Sikolsky (God bless his memory!) who was vainly trying to alert the nation to the folly of Social Security and Frances Perkins (the then Secretary of Labor) who was defending the swindle. *The Times* reported that Perkins ". . . sounded a warning last night against the Townsend plan, although she did not specify it by name . . ." *The Times* quoted Perkins as stating that ". . . contributory old age insurance, as provided in the Social Security Act, is not nearly as costly as an alternative of free pensions for old people in the country without regard to need . . .".[7]

The point is, the nation (in order to buy the scheme) was clearly being told by the Washington political establishment that Social Security was comparable to "old age insurance" and not at all like the "free pensions" then being urged upon the nation by the financial crack-pot Townsend. However, by comparison, today's Social Security program now makes Townsend look like a fiscal conservative!

[7] That debate (under the auspices of the League for Political Education) was broadcast nationally over the ABC Radio Network and emanated from Town Hall in New York City. Interest in the subject was so high that *The Times* reported, ". . . The crowd filled the auditorium and there were rows of standees at the rear, while a few late comers were turned away even though they had tickets. . ."

## Reserves To Finance Government Operations

Another *New York Times* article further reveals how the public perceived Social Security. This one appeared on April 3rd under the subcaption "Plan (Social Security) is for the Ultimate Financing Of The Government From Big Security Fund":

> "Payments into the Old Age Reserve account would carry an estimated average interest rate of 3 percent and it was explained that the government would come eventually to draw upon the reserve for financing its operations instead of through issuance of bonds and notes.
>
> Committee members hope to be able to show that interest for government money will thus go to the average citizen contribution to the old-age benefit fund instead of fiduciary investors.
>
> As for details of the *pension plan* contributors to the fund would not be eligible for old-age benefits until reaching 65, and no disbursements would be made before 1942. The minimum benefit to persons eligible to retire would be $15 a month and the maximum $25 a month. Their status would be determined according to whether an individual's earnings failed to reach or exceeded $3,000 during the period of his contributions.
>
> Actuarial considerations supplied the committee show that a total income of $4,000 during the contribution period would produce a monthly benefit of $15.83; and income of $6,000 $16.67; an income of $10,000, $20.83; and an income of $15,000, $25 a month.
>
> If an employee began contributing at the age of 20 and continued until he was 65 on an income of $2,000 annually, actuarial calculations are that he would be eligible for monthly benefits of $68.75." (emphasis added)

There is no question that Social Security was sold to the American public on the basis that it was to be a sound, actuarially funded "insurance" plan and not the unfunded "pay-as-you-go" Ponzi scheme it admittedly is today (see Figure 41). Indeed the public in 1935 was led to believe (by Congress) that the Social Security trust fund would be so huge that it would actually be used to support the Federal government[8] (not the other way around!), with the plan's participants earning the interest that the government customarily paid to its bond holders. Today, on the other hand, the public is warned that Social Security benefit payments may have to be subsidized and paid out of "general revenue".[9]

While the public began paying "into" Social Security in 1937, benefits did not begin until January 1, 1942.[10] The reason for the 5 year delay was to create the illusion that a "reserve" was being built up from which benefits were to be paid.

## The $64,000 Question

Today, 36,000,000 Americans (approximately 15% of the population) receive Social Security checks each

[8] It did, but not in a manner understood or contemplated by the public. See pages 217-218, Appendix A.

[9] There is, of course, no other source out of which Social Security payments can be made. So such "warnings" are totally misleading.

[10] The first Social Security check #00-000-001 for $22.54 was sent to Miss Ida M. Fuller, a bookkeeper/secretary from Ludlow, Vermont. Miss Fuller started to pay Social Security taxes in 1937. In 1950 she received her first increase and her new check amounted to $41.30. As of 1974 her check was $105.00 per month after deductions for medicare and she had passed her 100th birthday. In January, 1975 she received her last check of $109.27. Over the years Miss Fuller collected $20,000 in Social Security benefits. She paid in only $22.50.

month from the Federal government. Suppose in 1935 the U.S. Congress had proposed immediately putting the same proportion of the nation on Social Security, drawing comparable benefits to those received by today's recipients. This would have meant immediately sending 19,000,000 Americans Social Security checks (or 15% of America's 1935 population of 127,000,000). How would such a proposition have been received by the nation in 1935? Anyone proposing such an idea would have been looked upon as a complete screwball! Why? The public would have asked, "How could such commitments be met? There is no trust fund out of which such benefits can be paid!"

WELL, THERE IS NO "TRUST FUND" TODAY OUT OF WHICH CURRENT SOCIAL SECURITY PAYMENTS CAN BE PAID, SO IF IT WOULD HAVE MADE NO SENSE IN 1935 TO IMMEDIATELY PUT 19,000,000 AMERICANS ON A PUBLIC DOLE (DRAWING SOCIAL SECURITY BENEFITS COMPARABLE TO THOSE RECEIVED BY TODAY'S RECIPIENTS), IT CERTAINLY DOESN'T MAKE ANY SENSE TO DO THE SAME THING TODAY! How long will we allow this madness to continue?

## SUMMARIZING THE POINTS COVERED IN CHAPTER 6

1. Social Security was sold to the nation in 1935 as "Old Age Insurance" and *not* as a pay-as-you-go scheme.
2. The "insurance reserve" projected by 1980 was $50 billion which was then equivalent to 15 years of

federal receipts. In reality, by 1983 this "insurance reserve" was $2.6 billion *in the red.*[11]

3. Social Security "contributions" began in 1937 but benefits did not start until 1942. This created the illusion that benefits were being paid out of an accumulating "insurance reserve".
4. Today 36,000,000 (or 15% of the population) receive a monthly Social Security check and there is no "reserve" or "trust fund" to support these payments.
5. In 1935 Congress never would have passed (nor would the public have accepted) a bill which would send Social Security checks to 19,000,000 Americans since, at that time, there was obviously no "insurance" reserve from which such payments could be made. It is not any more legal — nor makes any more sense — to do the same thing today!

[11] And had an unfunded liability in excess of $5 trillion — or five times bigger than the reported national debt. See pages 89–91, *The Biggest Con.*

# 7

# An Analysis Of Government Studies: Proof That Government Cannot Be Trusted

In January, 1983 the National Committee on Social Security Reform (established by President Reagan on December 16, 1981) issued its long-awaited report. Commenting on the Committee's recommendations in his State of the Union message, President Reagan noted that, "As 1983 began the system (Social Security) stood on the brink of disaster . . .". He then proceeded to assure the nation that Committee members had apparently submerged their own political differences to come up with recommendations that could "save Social Security".

Commenting on the President's remarks in the March, 1983 issue of *The Schiff Report,* I said: "He (Reagan) encouraged the nation to believe that this pyramid scheme could be 'saved'. He took special pride in pointing out that 'pundits and experts predicted that the party divisions and conflicting interests would prevent the commission from agreeing on a plan to save Social Security.' Since Social Security is nothing but a chain letter, the Commission's plan to 'save' the system amounted to nothing more than a scheme to get more immediate chain so the politicians could postpone the day when that which must inevitably hit the fan, hits the fan!"

President Reagan's "Committee" was but another government committee in a long line of committees that have, over the years, sought to "save" or "strengthen" Social Security, but to no avail. Despite numerous "hearings", studies and reports, President Reagan stated that as of the beginning of 1983 Social Security "stood on the brink of disaster". This particular Committee's report and suggestions will prove to be no more helpful in "saving" Social Security than were prior committees and reports. All the latest report does is confirm the uselessness (as far as the public is concerned) of government committees, since the only sensible conclusions this committee could have reached (based upon its own findings) were: 1) Social Security is over; 2) this politically inspired socialistic experiment is a failure; 3) the sooner the public realizes it, the better off the nation will be; 4) terminating this "experiment" will undoubtedly create hardships, but that these hardships cannot be avoided; and 5) the longer the nation persists in believing that Social Security is viable, the greater the ultimate injury to the nation will be.

Such conclusions are inescapable! Look at just a few of the many charts and tables which this study produced. Figures 26, 27, 28 and 29 are reproductions of the graphs that appear on pages 24, 25, 26 and 29 (statement 7) of the Committee's report. Given these graphs, is there anybody in his right mind who can still believe this "program" can be "saved"? The growth rate of Social Security expenditures now appears virtually as a *straight vertical line,* shooting right up into the ionosphere!

Figure 27 shows that between 1942 and 1955 expenditures increased at a gradual, 5% rate. By 1955 the rate increased to 10%. By 1965 the rate had reached 30% and, by 1970, benefit reductions were obviously required in order to restrain this disastrous rate of accelerating Social Security payments. But what action did our lawmakers take? Instead of adopting measures to retard this obviously unacceptable rate of increasing expenditures, they actually adopted measures which would accelerate it! Sure enough, by 1970, the rate reached 70% and by 1980 it had climbed to 75%!

## The U.S. Congress Acts (Ineffectively) Only When A Crisis Develops

The table on page (7)-29 (Figure 29) shows that by 1983 the OASI trust fund was short $2.6 billion, while the other two "funds" only had $19 billion, or enough to last 8 weeks. Even though the U.S. Congress finally passed legislation (in 1983) to modestly reduce Social Security benefits, it is important for the public to understand that it did so only *after* the OASI Fund had *completely run out of money!* This is proof that the U.S. Congress never acts to *prevent* a problem from happening but, rather, acts only after the problem has reached crisis proportions.[1] These cuts, incidentally, were far

[1] The same situation occurred in connection with the so-called "energy crisis" which the Federal government created. This "crisis" was predictable (and thus preventable) long before the 1973 gas lines. See Chapter 6 of *The Biggest Con,* "The Energy Crisis — How the U.S. Government Planned It".

## FIGURE 26

TOTAL ANNUAL EXPENDITURES
*OASI AND*DI PROGRAMS COMBINED

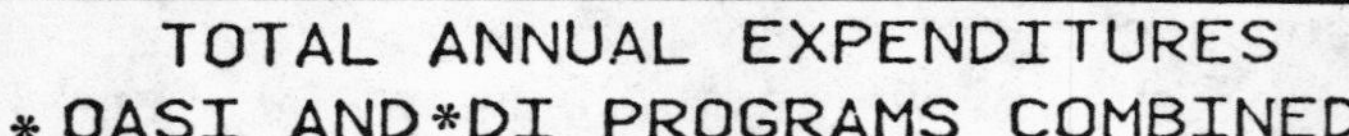

BILLIONS OF DOLLARS
240
220
200
180
160
140
120
100
80
60
40
20
1
1950
1955
1960
1965
1970
1975
1980
1985
COST-OF-LIVING ADJUSTMENTS 1974 AND AFTER
51.8 PERCENT CUMULATIVE BENEFIT INCREASE 1970-1972
DISABILITY BENEFITS 1957

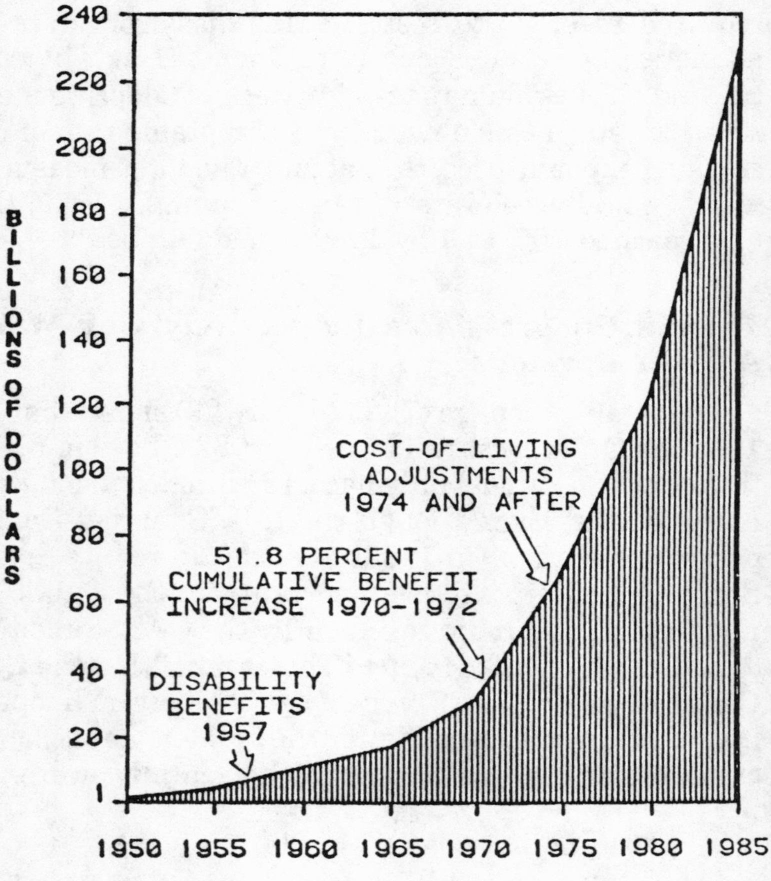

NOTE: 1985 BASED ON INTERMEDIATE PROJECTIONS

Statement (7), page 24

*** OASI refers to Old/Age Survivors Insurance and DI refers to Disability Insurance.**

# FIGURE 27

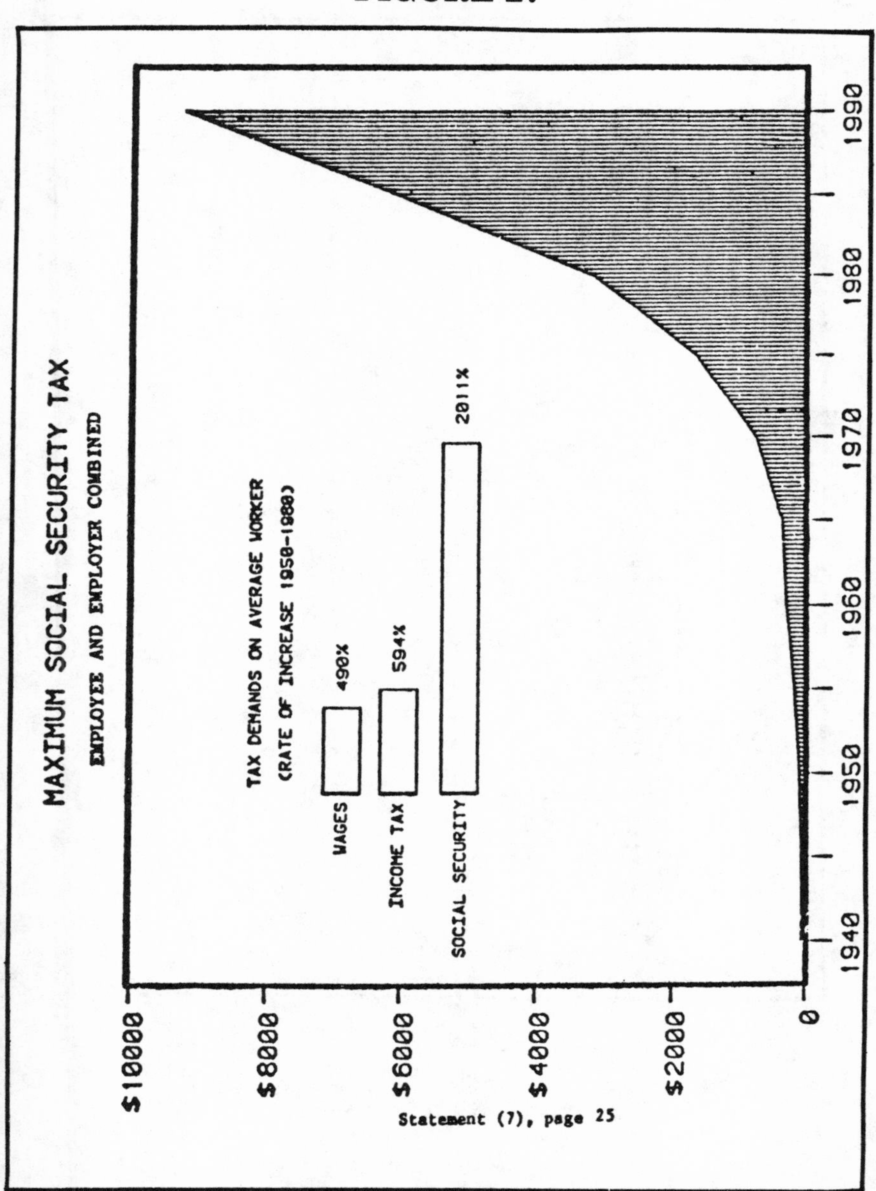
MAXIMUM SOCIAL SECURITY TAX
EMPLOYEE AND EMPLOYER COMBINED
TAX DEMANDS ON AVERAGE WORKER
(RATE OF INCREASE 1950-1980)
WAGES
490%
INCOME TAX
594%
SOCIAL SECURITY
2011%
1940
1950
1960
1970
1980
1990
$10000
$8000
$6000
$4000
$2000
0
Statement (7), page 25

## FIGURE 28

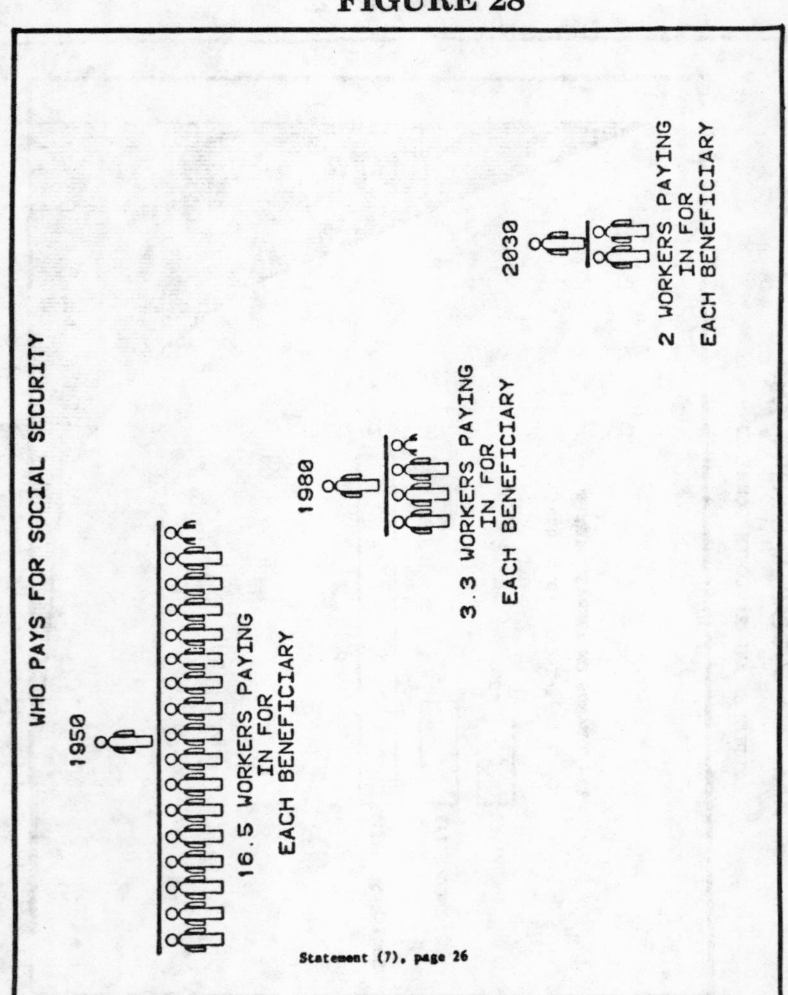


Statement (7), page 26

# FIGURE 29

## A Social Security Fact Sheet

Here, as supplied by the Social Security Administration, are some pertinent facts on social security's recipients, its taxpayers and its financial health.

### NUMBER OF BENEFICIARIES

| | 1972 | 1977 | April 1982 |
|---|---|---|---|
| Old age and survivors trust fund | 25,204,542 | 29,228,350 | 31,808,503 |
| Disability trust fund | 3,271,486 | 4,854,206 | 4,337,195 |

### AVERAGE MONTHLY BENEFIT

| | 1972 | 1977 | Sept. 1982 |
|---|---|---|---|
| Retired worker | $157 | $237 | $405 |
| Retired worker and aged spouse | 273 | 404 | 692 |
| Widowed mother, two children | 383 | 547 | 925 |
| Disabled worker | 175 | 266 | 429 |
| Disabled worker and family | 363 | 538 | 869 |

### SOCIAL SECURITY PAYROLL TAXES

The tax rate is for both employers and employees, and the increases shown are already scheduled; the wage base is indexed under the law, and increases assume moderate economic growth.

| | Tax rate | Wage base | Maximum contribution |
|---|---|---|---|
| 1972 | 5.20% | $9,000 | $468 |
| 1977 | 5.85 | 16,500 | 965 |
| 1982 | 6.70 | 32,400 | 2,171 |
| 1983 | 6.70 | 35,100 | 2,352 |
| 1984 | 6.70 | 37,500 | 2,513 |
| 1985 | 7.05 | 40,500 | 2,855 |
| 1986 | 7.15 | 43,800 | 3,132 |
| 1987 | 7.15 | 46,800 | 3,346 |
| 1988 | 7.15 | 50,100 | 3,582 |
| 1989 | 7.15 | 53,400 | 3,818 |
| 1990 | 7.65 | 57,000 | 4,361 |

### CASH OUTLAYS

(Calendar years, billions of dollars)

| | 1972 | 1977 | 1982 (est.) |
|---|---|---|---|
| Old age | $38.5 | $75.3 | $141.9 |
| Disability | 4.7 | 11.9 | 18.1 |

### TRUST FUND RESERVES

Reserves (in billions) are shown for the old age and survivors, disability and hospital insurance funds; fund ratios—money on hand at the beginning of a year as a fraction of the amounts needed for the full year—are for old age and survivors combined with disability, and for all three funds combined.

| | Year-end reserves | | | Fund ratios | |
|---|---|---|---|---|---|
| | * OASI | * DI | * HI | OASDI | OASDHI |
| 1972 | $35.3 | $7.5 | — | 93% | — |
| 1977 | 32.5 | 3.4 | — | — | — |
| 1982 | 17.3 | 1.6 | $15.8 | 15 | 22% |
| 1983 | ↘ -2.6 | 8.7 | 19.0 | 11 | 16 |
| 1984 | -26.4 | 18.4 | 21.0 | 3 | 10 |
| 1985 | -50.0 | 34.6 | 23.6 | -4 | 5 |
| 1986 | -77.6 | 53.8 | 28.0 | -7 | 3 |

Statement (7), page 29

*** OASI refers to Old/Age Survivors Insurance; DI refers to Disability Insurance; and HI refers to Hospital Insurance.**

too little and came far too late to be of any real help in "saving" this basket case.

*Useless Government Committees*

An analysis of government hearings and reports with respect to Social Security is included in this chapter to provide clear, unassailable proof that the American public cannot, in any way, trust the United States Congress or any of its committees. This, of course, applies equally to the executive branch of government. An analysis of these committee hearings and studies clearly suggests that the U.S. Congress is largely composed of incompetents, while the committees they create are composed of individuals who apparently haven't the foggiest idea of what they are studying or what the data they collect means.[2]

Based upon the following admission by Senator Armstrong (one of the Committee members who also serves as Chaïrman of the Senate subcommittee on Social Security), no other conclusion is possible.

*The Committee's Most Important "Achievement"*

"The most important single achievement of the Commission," said Armstrong, "under the patient considerate and scholarly leadership of Chairman Greenspan, has been to marshall a concensus for *admitting the problem*". To provide confirmation for his incisive

[2] And it apparently makes no difference which political party is in control. From a practical standpoint there is about as much political difference between Democrats and Republicans as there is between the New York Yankees and the Boston Red Sox. Some differences have to be manufactured, of course, otherwise the political game could not be played at all.

observation, Armstrong quotes the *Washington Post* as saying, "The first step toward solving any problem is to get people to admit the problem exists. The National Commission on Social Security Reform, meeting this week in Washington, has already made a *huge contribution* by getting its members of different political persuasion to agree that Social Security problems are *real, urgent,* and within reason measurable."[3] (emphasis added in both quotes)

Well, if that was the Committee's *most important* "achievement", it certainly wasted a bundle of the taxpayer's money.[4] The OASI "trust fund", remember, was flat broke in October of 1982; and if that *single event* didn't prove to the U.S. Congress that Social Security problems were "real" and "urgent", then what do U.S. Congressmen use for brains?

## A More Accurate Study (At No Cost To Taxpayers) Was Available

Appendix B contains the entire Chapter 4 of my book, *The Biggest Con — How the Government is Fleecing You,* which I wrote in 1974 (published in 1976), and certainly qualifies as a "study" of Social Security. In addition, Appendix B contains the recommendation that I made concerning what (I believed) had to be done with Social Security at that time. Those recommendations are equally valid today. My analysis certainly proves the U.S. Congress should have known at least 10

[3] Report of the National Commission on Social Security Reform — January, 1983; pages 3 and 4, Statement (7).

[4] Committee's report cost taxpayers between $625,000 and $1.2 million, which was the projected cost of running the Committee for one year.

years ago that Social Security problems were "real" and "urgent" and that Congressional action was needed in order to prevent a looming problem from getting worse.

My 1974 study pointed out that Social Security liabilities for fiscal 1973 were $2.1 trillion and had increased over the previous year's liabilities by more than $300 billion. This one year's increase, I pointed out, exceeded the Federal government's entire revenue for that year! I also pointed out that Social Security's unfunded liabilities were 5 times greater than the entire reported national debt. If this didn't indicate a problem 10 years ago, I don't know what would. And, of course, if *I* figured out the problem in a matter of a few hours, why couldn't the Federal government (with all of its "experts") have done the same?

## *One Million Dollars To Prove The Obvious*

By 1973 it should have been obvious that the growth of Social Security expenditures was *already out of hand.* Why couldn't the U.S. Congress recognize or admit the problem 10 years ago and start to take responsible action then? The President has a Council of Economic Advisors who, in turn, have a large staff paid for by American taxpayers. Each branch of Congress has its own standing sub-committee on Social Security, and both houses participate in a Joint Committee on Economics which continually has had hearings on Social Security over the last 10 years. In addition, each year the Trustees of Social Security issue their own Annual Report. Yet, despite all this high-priced "talent", the U.S. Congress apparently didn't know the OASI "trust fund" would be dead broke by October 1982?!

## *Wasting The Taxpayer's Money*

Figures 30 - 35 are the full text taken from pages J-21, 22, 23, 25, 26 and 27 of the report. They deal with Social Security's "Long Range Cost Situation". The Committee apparently thought it vitally important to examine (in detail) Social Security's estimated income and outgo to the year *2050*. The Committee determined, for example, that the difference between income and outgo between the years 2045 and 2050 would be approximately .09/100 of 1% based on "alternative II-B" assumptions, as opposed to a gap of .94/100 of 1% using "alternative III" assumptions. Before reading this exciting stuff, you should also be aware of the following excerpt that appeared on page J-13 of the report which commented on a 1978 government report that made similar projections:

**Actual Experience in 1978-81 as Compared with Estimates Made in 1977**

The 1978 OASDI Trustees Report stated that the 1977 Amendments would "restore the financial soundness of the cash benefit program throughout the remainder of this century and into the early years of the next one." It was further stated that, beginning in 1981, the short-range and medium-range annual deficits of the trust funds would be eliminated. However, this did not occur — because of the adverse economic conditions during 1979-81, when prices rose more rapidly than wages and unemployment was substantially higher than anticipated (and despite the actual disability experience being more favorable than had been estimated to occur).

The intermediate cost estimates for the OASDI Trust Funds that were made in 1977 for the law as then amended showed decreases in the fund balance in 1978-80 (a total drop of $8.0 billion), but a significant build-up in 1981 ($7.4 billion). In actuality, there were decreases of $9.4 billion in 1978-80 and of $1.9 billion in 1981. The pessimistic estimate made in 1977 showed that income and outgo would be in very close balance in 1981-84, but the actual economic conditions have been worse, so that a substantial deficit occurred in 1981 instead, and much larger ones apparently are ahead.

## FIGURE 30

**Long-Range Cost Situation**

The long-range financial status of the OASDI program will first be considered by looking at the estimated cost rates as compared with the combined . . . Appendix J, page 21

## FIGURE 31

. . . employer-employee tax rates, on a year-by-year basis. The National Commission has agreed that the long-range costs to be considered should be based on the intermediate cost estimate. The other cost estimates are discussed here so as to indicate the possible effect of alternative conditions.

Under the intermediate cost estimate, beginning in 1990 (when the OASDI tax rate is scheduled to increase significantly, and when a period of favorable demographic conditions is almost certain to occur[8]), the cost rates are smaller than the combined employer-employee tax rates (see Table 5). This situation continues for about the next two decades, with the excess generally ranging from about 1% to 1½% of taxable payroll. This period has been widely referred to as one when the program will be running large excesses of income over outgo and, as a result, building up large trust-fund balances.

A quite different picture is shown for the 1990s and early 2000s under the pessimistic cost estimate. The OASDI tax rate

## FIGURE 31 (continued)

during the 1990s and early 2000s falls short of the cost rate each year by about ½% of taxable payroll (see Table 5). Corresponding figures for the optimistic (Alternative I) estimate are not shown in Table 5 on a year-by-year basis, but they are shown for 25-year periods in Table 6; under this estimate, the OASDI tax rate during the 1990s and early 2000s exceeds the cost rate each year by about 3% of taxable payroll.

Appendix J, page 22

## FIGURE 32

Table 5

ESTIMATED COST RATES OF OASDI PROGRAM UNDER ALTERNATIVES II-B AND III AND COMPARISON WITH TAX RATES, 1982-2055
(as percent of taxable payroll)

| Calendar Year | OASDI Tax Rate[a/] | Alternative II-B Cost Rate | Alternative II-B Difference[b/] | Alternative III Cost Rate | Alternative III Difference[b/] |
|---|---|---|---|---|---|
| 1982 | 10.80% | 11.78% | -.98% | 11.83% | -1.03% |
| 1985 | 11.40 | 11.70 | -.30 | 12.40 | -1.00 |
| 1990 | 12.40 | 11.64 | +.76 | 12.85 | -.45 |
| 1995 | 12.40 | 11.42 | +.98 | 12.97 | -.57 |
| 2000 | 12.40 | 11.03 | +1.37 | 12.82 | -.42 |
| 2005 | 12.40 | 10.95 | +1.45 | 12.97 | -.57 |
| 2010 | 12.40 | 11.53 | +.87 | 13.92 | -1.52 |
| 2015 | 12.40 | 12.82 | -.42 | 15.76 | -3.36 |
| 2020 | 12.40 | 14.44 | -2.04 | 18.17 | -5.77 |
| 2025 | 12.40 | 15.97 | -3.57 | 20.70 | -8.30 |
| 2030 | 12.40 | 16.83 | -4.43 | 22.63 | -10.23 |
| 2035 | 12.40 | 17.02 | -4.62 | 23.94 | -11.54 |
| 2040 | 12.40 | 16.80 | -4.40 | 24.80 | -12.40 |
| 2045 | 12.40 | 16.66 | -4.26 | 25.80 | -13.40 |
| 2050 | 12.40 | 16.72 | -4.32 | 26.93 | -14.53 |
| 2055 | 12.40 | 16.81 | -4.41 | 27.87 | -15.47 |

## FIGURE 32 (continued)

| | | | | | |
|---|---|---|---|---|---|
| Averages | | | | | |
| 1982-2006 | 12.01 | 11.37 | +.64 | 12.73 | -.72 |
| 2007-31 | 12.40 | 14.08 | -1.68 | 17.84 | -5.44 |
| 2032-56 | 12.40 | 16.81 | -4.41 | 25.66 | -13.26 |
| 1982-2056 | 12.27 | 14.09 | -1.82 | 18.74 | -6.47 |

a/ For employer and employee combined.

b/ Tax rate minus cost rate. Positive differences are referred to as cash-flow surpluses, and negative differences as deficits.

NOTE: These estimates do not take into account the effect of the Tax Equity and Fiscal Responsibility Act of 1982 (P.L. 97-248). If this had been done, the cost rates would have been slightly lower.

SOURCE: Tables 27 and 29 of the 1982 OASDI Trustees Report.

Appendix J, page 23

## FIGURE 33

In the period following 2010, under the intermediate cost estimate, the OASDI tax rate tends to fall short of the cost rate by an increasing margin — beginning in 2030, by almost 4½% of taxable payroll. Under the pessimistic cost estimate, the excess of the cost rate over the tax rate steadily increases, until it reaches somewhat over 15% of taxable payroll. On the other hand, under the optimistic cost estimate, the OASDI tax rate exceeds the cost rate until about 2025; it is lower for the next 10 years, but once again is higher (by about 1% of taxable payroll at the end of the 75-year valuation period).

Over the entire 75-year valuation period, the average OASDI cost rate exceeds the average combined employer-employee tax rate by 1.82% of taxable payroll in the intermediate cost estimate of the 1982 Trustees Report (see Table 6).[9] It may be noted that 1.82% of the total taxable payroll in 1982 was about $25 billion per year.

## FIGURE 33 (continued)

The long-range actuarial imbalance is almost 6½% of taxable payroll under pessimistic cost estimate. The optimistic cost estimate (Alternative I) shows a favorable actuarial balance of 1.29% of taxable payroll, while the more optimistic of the two intermediate cost estimates (Alternative II-A) shows an actuarial deficiency of .82% of taxable payroll.

When successive 25-year periods are considered, the intermediate cost estimate for the OASDI program shows a small positive balance (.64% of taxable . . .

Appendix J, page 25

## FIGURE 34

. . . payroll) for the first period. This occurs because the "deficits" of income over outgo in the 1980s are more than offset by the "surpluses" following 1990 (and up through 2006). Increasingly larger deficits are shown for the next two 25-year periods — 1.68% of taxable payroll for the second period and 4.41% of taxable payroll for the third period. The deficit in the second period is 12% of the average cost rate (which means that, if benefit outgo were to be decreased sufficiently to be financed by the average tax rate, a reduction of 12% would be necessary). The deficit for the third period is 26% of the average cost of rate.

When the first 50-year period is considered as a whole, there is a "deficit" of income over outgo of .52% of taxable payroll for the OASDI program, according to the intermediate cost estimate. The corresponding figure for the pessimistic cost estimate is a "deficit" of 3.08% of taxable payroll, while under the optimistic estimate, there is a "surplus" of 1.68% of taxable payroll.

## FIGURE 34 (continued)

It is important to note that, if an economic stabilizing mechanism (such as is described in Chapter 2) were in effect in the 1990s and after, then the adverse results shown for present law under the pessimistic cost estimate would not occur. Rather, there would be excesses of tax income over outgo for benefit payments and administrative expenses throughout the period.

The estimated significant annual excesses of the OASDI tax rate over the cost rate in the 1990s and early 2000s result in a sizable build-up of . . .

Appendix J, page 26

## FIGURE 35

. . . trust-fund assets under the intermediate cost estimate (assuming that, in the 1980s, the deficits occurring then were financed in some manner, even though they might be repaid later). Table 7 indicates that a fund ratio of about 180% is estimated to occur between 2010 and 2015, but thereafter it decreases rapidly until the fund would be exhausted shortly after 2025. Under the pessimistic cost estimate, the OASDI fund ratio would never become positive, because the cost rates always exceed the tax rates. Quite naturally, under the more optimistic of the cost estimates, the cost rates are lower than the tax rates in almost all years after 1990, and so the fund ratio increases steadily over the 75-year valuation period.

After admitting that a prior government committee was *totally off the mark* in predicting Social Security receipts only 3 years away, the Committee (in all seriousness) proceeded to examine Social Security income and outgo until the year 2050! Why didn't the Committee understand that it could have, with equal logic, issued a report speculating on how many angels could dance on the head of a pin!?

Now we read even more exciting stuff, reported verbatim from pages J-27, 28, 29, 30 and 31 of the Report (Figures 36 — 40).

## FIGURE 36

**Effect of the Real-Wage Differential**

Perhaps the most significant economic factor affecting costs in the actuarial estimates for the OASDI program is the real-wage differentia!, which is (1) the annual percentage increase in wages and salaries in covered employment, minus (2) the annual percentage increase in the CPI(W). The assumptions for the differential are based primarily on a projection of historical trends, which in turn reflect productivity gains and the factors that link such gains with the real-wage differential. Such differential has a direct effect on the cost estimates, but the associated assumptions for productivity gains and the factors linking such gains with the real-wage differential (as discussed in the next paragraph) do *not* have a direct effect on the long-range cost estimates expressed as a percentage of taxable payroll.

Appendix J, page 27

## FIGURE 37

### Table 7

ESTIMATED TRUST FUND RATIOS BY ALTERNATIVE AND TRUST FUND, CALENDAR YEARS 1982-2060

| Calendar year | Alternative I | | | Alternative II-A | | | Alternative II-B | | | Alternative III | | |
|---|---|---|---|---|---|---|---|---|---|---|---|---|
| | OASI | DI | Total | OASI | DI | Total | OASI | DI | Total | OASI | DI | Total |
| 1982 | * 15 | 16 | 15 | 15 | 16 | 15 | 15 | 16 | 15 | 15 | 16 | 15 |
| 1983 | 10 | 8 | 10 | 10 | 8 | 10 | 11 | 8 | 10 | 11 | 8 | 11 |
| 1984 | 1 | 48 | 6 | (¹) | 47 | 4 | (²) | 43 | 3 | (²) | 39 | 1 |
| 1985 | -7 | 98 | 4 | -11 | 93 | (¹) | (²) | 84 | -4 | (²) | 71 | (²) |
| 1986 | -10 | 178 | 9 | -18 | 169 | (²) | (²) | 148 | -7 | (²) | 125 | (²) |
| 1987 | -10 | 265 | 17 | -24 | 253 | 3 | (²) | 217 | -10 | (²) | 181 | (²) |
| 1988 | -9 | 359 | 27 | -28 | 342 | 8 | (²) | 288 | -13 | (²) | 239 | (²) |
| 1989 | -6 | 464 | 40 | -30 | 432 | 15 | (²) | 361 | -16 | (²) | 297 | (²) |
| 1990 | (²) | 567 | 56 | -32 | 524 | 22 | (²) | 436 | -19 | (²) | 356 | (²) |
| 1991 | 15 | 696 | 82 | -26 | 642 | 39 | (²) | 536 | -13 | (²) | 436 | (²) |
| 1992 | 31 | 811 | 110 | -18 | 753 | 58 | (²) | 631 | -7 | (²) | 509 | (²) |
| 1993 | 47 | 934 | 138 | -10 | 859 | 77 | (²) | 723 | (²) | (²) | 577 | (²) |
| 1994 | 65 | 1,041 | 167 | (¹) | 961 | 97 | (²) | 812 | 7 | (²) | 643 | (²) |
| 1995 | 84 | 1,137 | 197 | 8 | 1,054 | 116 | (²) | 895 | 15 | (²) | 705 | (²) |
| 1996 | 104 | 1,208 | 228 | 18 | 1,122 | 136 | (²) | 959 | 23 | (²) | 755 | (²) |
| 1997 | 127 | 1,278 | 260 | 29 | 1,187 | 157 | (²) | 1,019 | 32 | (²) | 799 | (²) |
| 1998 | 150 | 1,345 | 293 | 41 | 1,247 | 178 | (²) | 1,076 | 42 | (²) | 837 | (²) |
| 1999 | 175 | 1,411 | 326 | 52 | 1,317 | 200 | (²) | 1,130 | 53 | (²) | 871 | (²) |
| 2000 | 202 | 1,468 | 362 | 67 | 1,369 | 223 | (²) | 1,178 | 64 | (²) | 900 | (²) |
| 2001 | 232 | 1,532 | 400 | 82 | 1,421 | 247 | (²) | 1,227 | 76 | (²) | 927 | (²) |
| 2002 | 262 | 1,589 | 438 | 99 | 1,467 | 271 | (²) | 1,270 | 89 | (²) | 951 | (²) |
| 2003 | 293 | 1,630 | 474 | 116 | 1,502 | 295 | (²) | 1,303 | 102 | (²) | 967 | (²) |
| 2004 | 324 | 1,656 | 510 | 133 | 1,526 | 317 | (²) | 1,327 | 115 | (²) | 977 | (²) |
| 2005 | 354 | 1,656 | 542 | 149 | 1,531 | 338 | (²) | 1,332 | 128 | (²) | 976 | (²) |
| 2006 | 384 | 1,702 | 576 | 165 | 1,568 | 358 | (²) | 1,366 | 140 | (²) | 991 | (²) |

## FIGURE 37 (continued)

| | | | | | | | | | | | | |
|---|---|---|---|---|---|---|---|---|---|---|---|---|
| 2010 | 485 | 1,797 | 684 | 216 | 1,645 | 419 | (2) | 1,435 | 177 | (2) | 1,005 | (2) |
| 2015 | 539 | 1,967 | 745 | 224 | 1,779 | 434 | (2) | 1,549 | 177 | (2) | 1,033 | (2) |
| 2020 | 520 | 2,198 | 739 | 168 | 1,962 | 387 | (2) | 1,703 | 125 | (2) | 1,076 | (2) |
| 2025 | 457 | 2,549 | 698 | 67 | 2,240 | 300 | (2) | 1,938 | 31 | (2) | 1,162 | (2) |
| 2030 | 386 | 3,000 | 662 | (2) | 2,595 | 196 | (2) | 2,241 | (2) | (2) | 1,287 | (2) |
| 2035 | 332 | 3,410 | 651 | (2) | 2,902 | 89 | (2) | 2,504 | (2) | (2) | 1,390 | (2) |
| 2040 | 304 | 3,735 | 675 | (2) | 3,123 | (2) | (2) | 2,693 | (2) | (2) | 1,456 | (2) |
| 2045 | 298 | 4,031 | 719 | (2) | 3,295 | (2) | (2) | 2,837 | (2) | (2) | 1,515 | (2) |
| 2050 | 301 | 4,443 | 766 | (2) | 3,558 | (2) | (2) | 3,061 | (2) | (2) | 1,619 | (2) |
| 2055 | 305 | 4,942 | 811 | (2) | 3,873 | (2) | (2) | 3,330 | (2) | (2) | 1,758 | (2) |
| 2060 | 311 | 5,435 | 860 | (2) | 4,168 | (2) | (2) | 3,582 | (2) | (2) | 1,910 | (2) |
| Trust fund is projected to be first exhausted in: | 1983 | (4) | 1983 | 1983 | (4) | 1983 | 1983 | (4) | 1983 | 1983 | (4) | 1983 |

[1] Between -0.5 percent and zero.

[2] The fund is projected to be exhausted and not to recover before the end of the projection period.

[3] Between zero and 0.5 percent.

[4] The fund is not projected to be exhausted within the projection period.

Note: The ratios shown after the year in which a given fund is projected to be exhausted are theoretical and are shown for informational purposes only. In addition, the ratios for the total of the OASI and DI Trust Funds after 1982 are theoretical, because under the current law after 1982, the assets of one fund cannot be borrowed by another fund. The money assumed to be borrowed by the OASI Trust Fund in December 1982 is assumed to be repaid in 1992 under Alternative I, in 1998 under Alternative II-A, and not at any time in the long-range projection period under Alternatives II-B and III, although interest is assumed to be paid on a current basis. The assets used to compute the fund ratios are the gross assets, before taking into account the loans which occurred in 1982. If that had been done (i.e., considering the net assets), the OASI fund ratios would have been smaller, and the DI and HI fund ratios would have been larger.

Note: These estimates do not take into account the effect of the Tax Equity and Fiscal Responsibility Act of 1982 (P.L. 97-248). If this had been done, the fund ratios would have been slightly higher.

Source: Table 32 in 1982 OASDI Trustees Report.

Appendix J, page 28

## FIGURE 38

Such assumptions for productivity gains and the related linkage factors have been used, as a subsidiary procedure, to obtain estimates of the Gross National Product. Then, the long-range OASDI costs have then been expressed as a percentage of GNP. However, for the purpose of planning the financing of the OASDI program, by far the most important and critical measure is the relationship with taxable earnings, because the tax rates which finance the program are applied to such earnings.

The most important linkage factors between real-wage growth and productivity are the following: (1) relative growth of nontaxable fringe benefits as a proportion of total compensation, (2) the average number of hours worked per week, and (3) the average number of weeks worked per year. In the intermediate cost estimate (Alternative II-B), when GNP was estimated from the primary assumptions as to real-wage differentials, the result of the linkages was an ultimate (1992 and after) rate of productivity gains of 2.2% per year. This figure was derived from the real-wage differential of 1.5% per year by increasing it by .4% for the relative annual growth of fringe benefits, by .2% for the average number of hours worked per week, and by .1% for the average number of weeks worked per year (the net effect of other linkage factors than the three which were used was considered to be negligible).

Consideration of these two figures can lead to greatly different conclusions. On the one hand, it could be argued that the difference of .7% between productivity gains and real-wage growth is too large and that, . . .

Appendix J, page 29

## FIGURE 39

. . . therefore, the real-wage differential used should be higher than 1.5% — which would produce a considerably more favorable financial picture for the OASDI program than is currently estimated. On the other hand, it could be argued that the assumed ultimate productivity rate of 2.2% is too high and that then either (1) the several linkage factors are overstated, and the real-wage differential of 1.5% is satisfactory, or (2) the linkage factors are appropriate, but the real-wage differential should be lower than 1.5% — which would produce considerably less favorable financial picture for the OASDI program than currently estimated.

The estimates of GNP that have been derived from the basic actuarial estimates expressed as percentages of taxable payroll can be used to compare cost of the OASDI system with GNP. According to the intermediate cost estimate such cost is currently about 5.2% of GNP and will decrease slowly for the next 20 years, reaching a low of about 4.4%. It will increase to 6.1% in 2030, then again decline slowly, to about 5.5% at the end of the 75-year valuation period.

Under the pessimistic estimate, the cost of the OASDI program percentage of GNP remains relatively level at slightly more than 5% for the next 25 years, but it continuously increases thereafter to about 8.6% at the end of the valuation period. On the other hand, under the optimistic cost estimate (Alternative I), such ratio decreases slowly in the next few years, reaching a minimum of slightly less than 4% of GNP after 20 years and then slowly rise . . .

Appendix J, page 30

## FIGURE 40

. . . to somewhat more than 5% in the 2020s; thereafter, it decreases to somewhat less than 4½% ultimately.

Appendix J, page 31

GEE, IF GOVERNMENT EXPERTS CAN UNDERSTAND ALL THIS, WHY DIDN'T THEY UNDERSTAND THAT THE OASI "TRUST FUND" WOULD BE DEAD BROKE BY 1982?!

## One Picture Worth A Thousand Words

Proving the Chinese proverb that says "One Picture is Worth a Thousand Words" (or in the case of this report *50,000* words), I submit the Committee's own exhibit, "Who Pays for Social Security", which appeared on page (7)-26 of the report (see Figure 28).

Couldn't the Committee have figured out just from this one graph that there is no logical, legal or economic way that "2 or 2-½ or 3 or 3.3" Americans can be compelled to support another? Remember, in 1950 Social Security might have been palatable because such a recipient was being supported by 16-½ workers; but can the government force two American workers to support a third — when such workers might, themselves, not be able to afford a house, a car, or their own fuel bill? Such a conclusion doesn't require any particular expertise, just a little common sense. Yet this panel of "experts" wants the public to believe that such a situation is not only economically feasible but also legal!?

## Prior Government Committees and Studies

One need only examine the reports from a few government hearings to be fully convinced of the Federal government's culpability in connection with the Social Security fiasco. For example:

Testifying on May 27, 1976 before the Joint Economics Committee, W. Allen Wallis (Chancellor, University of Rochester and Chairman of the 1975 Advisory Council on Social Security) stated:

"Many people think that the Social Security taxes taken out of their wages and sent to Washington each month provide for their old-age pensions and other Social Security benefits. This simply is not the case. *Those taxes are levied on workers in order to pay benefits to people who already have retired and are drawing their Social Security pensions,* or to pay other Social Security benefits to those who already are drawing them . . . *When you pay Social Security taxes you are in no way making provision for your own retirement. You are paying the pensions of those who already are retired.*

Once you understand this, you see that whether you will get the benefits you are counting on when you retire depends on whether the Congress will levy enough taxes, borrow enough, *or print enough money,* and whether it will authorize the level of benefits you are counting on.

*The situation is in no way analogous to putting money each month into a private insurance company* which invests it and undertakes to pay you an annuity.

*Misunderstanding of the pay-as-you-go nature of Social Security is widespread among journalists and the public. 'Indeed, this misunderstanding seems to have been deliberately cultivated* sometimes, in the belief that it makes the Social Security System more palatable to the public."

(emphasis added)

Note how Wallis complains that "misunderstanding of the pay-as-you-go nature of Social Security is widespread among journalists and the public." Why are such misunderstandings so wide-spread? Why doesn't the public know the truth about Social Security? Well, Wallis himself supplies the answers. He says the "misunderstanding seems to have been deliberately cultivated. . .". By whom? By the government, of course!

The government knowingly and deliberately misled the public concerning a vital element in their financial future so Social Security would appear "more pallatable to them".

Wallis states that the "people think that the Social Security taxes taken out of (one's) wages are sent to Washington each month to provide for their old-age pensions. . .". Why wouldn't they think that? Look at those Social Security pamphlets on pages 227 and 228. The public is told in them that "Social Security contributions (go) into special trust funds" and that these "trust funds" are "soundly financed both for the short-range and long-range future". These government claims were, of course, *all lies* and were designed to "deliberately cultivate" the misconception to which Wallis refers. Should the culprits who deliberately cultivated these misconceptions go unpunished? What right did politicians and bureaucrats have to deliberately lie to the public in order to make Social Security "more pallatable"? The government's deliberate campaign to deceive the American public with respect to Social Security amounts to nothing less than *criminal* fraud.

### *Why Bother With A Securities and Exchange Commission?*

If the Federal government can tax the American public (imposing all types of burdens on capital-seeking entrepreneurs) to support a Securities and Exchange Commission (which presumably protects them from stock swindles), why should it be at liberty to swindle far more from this same public through its *own* "retirement" scam? Note again Wallis' reference to the "pay-as-you-go" nature of Social Security. Is this the type of Social Security "funding" that the Supreme Court had in mind when it held Social Security Constitutional[5] or what the nation had in mind when it bought the scheme?[6]

## Report Of The Quadrennial Advisory Council Of Social Security — March 10, 1975

Figures 41 and 42 are pages 45 and 46 of the 1975 Report of the Quadrennial Advisory Council of Social Security. Figure 43 is a list of the distinguished members and consultants who made up that Committee. Why didn't these "experts" honestly tell the American public (back in 1975) that Social Security was a scam and a fraud since that conclusion was inescapable from the evidence it had gathered?

Note the Committee's clear admission that Social Security merely (Figure 41, [a]) "transfers money from one generation to another with the amount taken from one generation being measured by the other generation's benefit requirements.". Therefore, Social Security taxes are *not* collected for the "general welfare of the United States" but, admittedly, are used to pay cash benefits to certain segments of society at the expense and to the exclusion of others. Is this what the government argued before the court? Is this the basis upon which the Supreme Court found Social Security constitutional?

And just who determines these "benefit requirements" anyway? The generation receiving the benefits? What legal argument can anyone advance to support the idea that one generation of Americans can

[5] See pages 163-165.

[6] See pages 102-105.

## FIGURE 41

The Chairman of the Council appointed a Subcommittee on Finance[1] to review the financial aspects of the social security system. It was assisted by five independent professionals, two economists and three actuaries. In the limited time available, the review was necessarily concentrated on the OASDI program because it faces financing difficulties. The report of the Subcommittee will be summarized in this chapter, but for additional information on any particular item, the reader is referred to the Subcommittee's detailed report which is attached as Appendix A.

### SECTION 1. BASIC CHARACTERISTICS OF OLD-AGE, SURVIVORS, AND DISABILITY INSURANCE PROGRAM

#### 1.1 CURRENT COST FINANCING

The financing of the OASDI system is based on the "current cost" method. Under this approach, no fund is created during the life of a worker from which his benefits are ultimately paid. Instead the social security taxes he pays are immediately paid out by the government to persons who are already beneficiaries. His own benefits will be paid from taxes that are collected in the future from persons who are then working. The tax rate is set so as to provide tax receipts that approximate current expenditures. In essence, the plan transfers money from one generation to another with the amount taken from the one generation being measured by the other generation's benefit requirements.

(a)

**FIGURE 41** (continued)

(b) The current cost method would be unacceptable for a private pension plan, but it is a sound alternative for OASDI, because the government has the continuing power to tax future workers in order to pay benefits in the future to those who are now working. (c) If OASDI were funded, in the actuarial sense, by creating a fund of one or two trillion dollars, that fund would have to be invested.[2] (d) The largest part would almost certainly go into government bonds because they are considered to be the safest investment. (e) The value of such bonds, however, depends on the power of the government to tax in the future. There would be, therefore, no really greater security behind the system than there is today, (f) but the funding would have a very real effect on capital formation in this country.

In fact, even with the current cost method, the OASDI system has affected the capital formation of the country and will continue to

[1] Members of the Subcommittee were Rudolph T. Danstedt, Elizabeth C. Norwood, and J. Henry Smith, with J. W. Van Gorkom as Chairman.

[2] By comparison, the Federal debt outstanding at the end of fiscal year 1974 held by the public is estimated to be about $360 billion.

(45)

## FIGURE 42

affect it in ways that are not clearly understood at this time. Since the formation of adequate capital for the nation's needs is a currently pressing problem, the Council strongly recommends that a study of the relationship between the financing of the social security system and capital formation be made at the earliest possible time.

### 1.2 MEASURING LONG-RANGE COSTS

In discussing the "cost" of the OASDI system, the use of numbers in absolute dollars is of little help, because there are constant changes in the number of workers, beneficiaries, wage and benefit levels and other factors. Throughout this report, therefore, we will be expressing "cost" as a percentage of total covered earnings, meaning earnings subject to the OASDI tax. This is the measure of cost that will be used herein because it focuses attention on the size of the burden to be borne by each individual taxpayer and employer. As an example, the cost of the system in 1975 was 10.67 percent of covered earnings. Since total covered earnings in 1974 approximated $600 billion, absolute cost of the system in that year was around $64 billion.

### 1.3 OASDI TAX RATES

The current tax rate for OASDI is 9.9 percent, payable on all earnings up to $14,000.[3] The total tax is split equally between the employer and employee, with each paying 4.95 percent. (To this is added .9 percent for hospital insurance making a total social security tax of 5.85 percent borne by each.) The cash benefits tax rate for the self-employed was originally established at a level of 150 percent of the employee's tax. However, in recent years it has been frozen at 7 percent.

**FIGURE 42** (continued)

### 1.4 WEIGHTED BENEFIT STRUCTURE

While the tax rate for all employees is the same, the benefits are not equal. They are weighted in favor of lower-paid workers and those with dependents. The low-paid worker receives a benefit that is a higher percentage of his (or her) average earnings than does the higher-paid employee, even though the latter receives a larger absolute amount. This weighting of the benefit schedule represents society's recognition of "adequacy" as a criterion of the plan, and is a departure from the strict principle of individual equity. Another such social concept is found in the fact that a married worker receives certain protection for his dependents without paying any more premium than a single worker who receives no such protection. ← **(g)**

The entire social security program is necessarily a blend of social goals and individual equity. Maintaining the proper blend is very important if we are to sustain the workers' support of the plan. To date, most workers feel responsible for the system because, while aware of the social weighting within the program, they still view their protection as being reasonably related to the taxes they pay. This attitude is important to the success of social security. It becomes an important factor when considering the introduction of additional welfare-type benefits or methods of financing from general revenues. ← **(h)**

[3] The $14,000 applies to earnings of 1975. The amount rises each year in accordance with the increase in average wages in covered employment.

## FIGURE 43

### MEMBERSHIP OF THE COUNCIL

*W. Allen Wallis, Chairman,* Rochester, New York, Chancellor of the University of Rochester, and a former special assistant to President Eisenhower.

*Stanford D. Arnold,* Brighton, Michigan, Secretary-Treasurer, Michigan State Building and Construction Trades Council, AFL–CIO.

*John W. Byrnes,* Arlington, Virginia. Attorney; former U.S. Representative from Wisconsin and former ranking minority member of the House Ways and Means Committee.

*Rita Ricardo Campbell,* Los Altos Hills, California, Senior Fellow, Hoover Institution, Stanford University; former member of President's Committee on Health Service Industry.

*Edward J. Cleary,* Flushing, New York. Secretary-Treasurer, New York State Building and Construction Trades Council, AFL–CIO.

*Rudolph T. Danstedt,* Bethesda, Maryland. Assistant to the President of the National Council of Senior Citizens.

*Edwin J. Faulkner,* Lincoln, Nebraska. President, Woodmen Accident and Life Company.

*Vernon E. Jordan, Jr.,* White Plains, New York. Executive Director, National Urban League. (Mr. Jordan was unable to participate in the Council's work and was represented by Thomas E. Mitchell, Washington, D.C., Deputy Director, Washington Bureau, National Urban League.)

*Elizabeth C. Norwood,* Washington, D.C. Assistant Research Director, Eastern Conference of Teamsters.

**FIGURE 43** (continued)

*John J. Scanlon*, Fairfield, Connecticut. Executive Vice President and Chief Financial Officer (Ret.), American Telephone and Telegraph Company.

*J. Henry Smith*, Maplewood, New Jersey. Chairman of the Board, Equitable Life Assurance Society of the United States.

*J. W. Van Gorkom*, Lake Forest, Illinois. President, Trans Union Corporation.

*Arnold R. Weber*, *Vice Chairman*, Pittsburgh, Pennsylvania. Dean, Graduate School of Industrial Administration, Carnegie-Mellon University; former Assistant Secretary, Department of Labor: former Associate Director, Office of Management and Budget.

**CONSULTANTS TO THE COUNCIL**

*Philip Cagan*, Professor of Economics, Columbia University.

*Hugh Conway*, Economist, Office of the Secretary of Labor.

*Martin Feldstein*, Professor of Economics, Harvard University.

*Robert Kaplan*, Professor of Industrial Administration, Carnegie-Mellon University.

*Robert J. Myers*, Professor of Actuarial Science, Temple University; former Chief Actuary, Social Security Administration.

*Sherwin Rosen*, Professor of Economics, University of Rochester.

*Charles E. Trowbridge*, Senior Vice President and Chief Actuary, The Bankers Life; former Chief Actuary, Social Security Administration.

*Howard Young*, Consulting Actuary; Special Consultant to the President, United Auto Workers.

legally compel another generation to supply it with what it thinks it "needs"? Is it based on the premise that the *next* generation will supply *that* generation with what *it* thinks *it* needs?! How could a panel of "experts" come up with such a ludicrous thesis? But wait . . . it gets worse!

## Current Cost Financing

"The current cost method would be unacceptable for a private pension" we are told, (Figure 41, [b]) "but it is a sound alternative for OASDI because the government has the continuing power to tax future workers in order to pay benefits in the future for those who are now working.". More proof that Social Security taxes are not levied "for the general welfare of the United States"! This statement alone proves that apparently no one on that committee had the foggiest idea of what they were talking about. For one thing "current cost funding" means that *no funding whatsoever* takes place![7] All the money that comes in, goes out. Oh, some of it might stay in the goverment's checking account for a month or so, but that hardly constitutes "funding"! On this basis defense spending can be said to be "current cost funded" as well as the spending for the Justice Department and the S.E.C. Does the government make gradiose claims that the S.E.C., the Justice Department and all other government departments and agencies are equally "current cost funded"? The development of "current cost funding" was obviously done to confuse the public into believing that "funding" was taking place when

[7] Funding means to set money aside out of which a future liability can be paid. Since no money is being set aside to be used later, no "financing" or "funding" can be said to take place.

such was not the case. It illustrates the lengths to which the Federal government will go in order to delude the public as to what is really going on.

The Committee employs this concept so the public and the media can continue to be fooled. What the Committee should have said is, "Social Security is *not funded on any basis whatsoever,* and all talk of 'funding' has no more relevance to Social Security than it has to defense spending or the F.B.I. So let's drop all pretenses that Social Security is 'financed' or 'funded' on any basis whatsoever. Such terms have no meaning when applied to Social Security and can only contribute to the public's confusion regarding the program." The Committee should have said, "Money comes in and money goes out —*period* and the government will hope and pray that it can continue to coerce the public into paying what the politicians have irresponsibly promised."[8]

## This Book Explodes Another Committee Misconception

Of course, this book knocks into a cocked hat the committee's belief that while "the current cost method would be unacceptable for a private pension (it) is a sound alternative for OASDI because the government has the continuing power to tax future workers. . ."

[8] The 1983 Report put it this way — "Over the years, the original emphasis on building up and maintaining a large fund was reduced. Gradually, the funding basis shifted, in practice, to what might be called a current-cost or pay-as-you-go basis. The intent under such a basis is that income and outgo should be approximately equal each year. . . .".

This book proves[9] that the government has no such power *once the public discovers the truth* and learns how to stop paying! Since this book will undoubtedly cause millions of Americans to stop paying Social Security taxes, the Committee's admission proves and establishes that "current cost funding" is *not* a *valid alternative* and, therefore, Social Security cannot be responsible (on *any* basis) for saving Americans "from the rigors of the poor house" — the very basis upon which the program was illegally found to be constitutional.

The Committee's comments on the "trust funds" themselves are also illuminating. The Committee states that if Social Security collections were, indeed, invested in trust funds, these trust funds would have to be (Figure 41, [c]) "one or two trillion",[10] and would "almost certainly go into government bonds because they are considered to be the safest investment". (Figure 41, [d]). Considered safest by whom? The reason that they would have to go into government bonds is that *by law* that is the only "investment" that can be made. Can the government buy stock in General Motors or IBM? Of course not! But a government's "investment" in its own "bonds" is no investment at all! (This is explained fully on page 217.)

## Committee Admits Social Security Founded on Fraud

Note, however, the Committee's comments (Figure 41, [e]) ridiculing the importance of a trust fund: "...

[9] Along with my other book, *How Anyone Can Stop Paying Income Taxes.*

[10] Social Security actuaries had already established that the unfunded liability in 1974 was $2.118 trillion. (See *The Biggest Con,* page 75) So the report that the trust funds would need an off-handed "one or two trillion" was an obvious attempt to minimize the amount the fund actually needed.

the value of such bonds, however, depends on the power of the government to tax in the future and it would be, therefore, no really greater security behind the system than it is today.". In other words, the program is no better off with a "reserve" than it is without one. This simple statement explodes the myth originally promoted by the government concerning the value and reliability of a "gigantic" Social Security "reserve". And when the Committee states that a belief in a "reserve" made up of government bonds is actually an illusion, they are admitting that the government sold Social Security to the American public and to the courts on the strength of that illusion.

*All Government Trust Funds An Illusion*

The Committee's admission that government bonds held by the government amount to *having no bonds at all,* verifies that those programs backed by such "assets" are actually backed by nothing at all. Note, for example, Figure 44 which is an excerpt from the 1982 "Statement of Liabilities and Other Commitments of the United States Government" as of September 30, 1982. This schedule shows that as of that date the government claimed that various government agencies held approximately $208 billion of such "assets" supposedly as financial backing for various government projects. All such "bonds" (as the Committee explains) are meaningless, and merely deceive the public concerning the actual financial soundness of all of these programs. This report shows that the Federal Deposit Insurance Corporation owns $13.3 billion of such

## FIGURE 44

### Section I
### Schedule 2 - The Public Debt as of September 30, 1982
### (In millions)

| Public debt securities held by-- | Amount of public debt securities outstanding |
|---|---|
| Government accounts: | |
| Legislative Branch: | |
| Library of Congress | $86 |
| United States Tax Court: | |
| Tax Court judges survivors annuity fund | 1 |
| The Judiciary: | |
| Judicial survivors annuity fund | 73 |
| Funds appropriated to the President: | |
| Agency for International Development | 29 |
| Overseas Private Investment Corporation | 669 |
| Bequests and gifts--disaster relief | 1 |
| Department of Agriculture: | |
| Milk market orders assessment fund | 1 |
| Rural Telephone Bank | 3 |
| Reforestation trust fund | 106 |
| Other | * |
| Department of Commerce: | |
| Federal ship financing fund, revolving fund | 147 |
| Fishing vessel and gear damage compensation fund | 4 |
| War-risk insurance revolving fund | 10 |
| Gifts and bequests | * |
| Department of Defense: | |
| Department of Defense--Military | 5 |
| Department of Defense--civil: | |
| Inland waterways trust fund | 55 |
| * Department of Health and Human Services: | |
| ↑ Federal old-age and survivors insurance trust fund | 11,427 |
| Federal disability insurance trust fund | 6,753 |
| Federal hospital insurance trust fund | 20,800 |
| Federal supplementary medical insurance trust fund | 5,874 |
| Other | 13 |

**FIGURE 44** (continued)

| | |
|---|---|
| **Department of Housing and Urban Development:** | |
| Federal Housing Administration fund........... | $2,559 |
| Special assistance functions fund............. | 1 |
| Participation sales fund...................... | 1,143 |
| Guarantees of mortgage-backed securities fund | 379 |
| Low-rent public housing program............... | 20 |
| **Department of the Interior:** | |
| Deposits, Outer Continental Shelf Land Act.... | 4,807 |
| Indian tribal funds........................... | 335 |
| Preservation, birthplace of Abraham Lincoln... | * |
| Other......................................... | * |
| **Department of Labor:** | |
| Pension Benefit Guaranty Corporation.......... | 265 |
| Relief and rehabilitation, Longshoremen's and Harbor Workers' Compensation Acts as amended | 12 |
| Relief and rehabilitation, Workmen's Compensation Act within the District of Columbia.................................... | 1 |
| Unemployment trust fund....................... | 9,644 |
| **Department of State:** | |
| Foreign service retirement and disability fund | 1,190 |
| Conditional gift fund, general................ | 1 |
| **Department of Transportation:** | |
| Airport and airway trust fund................. | 3,868 |
| Aviation insurance revolving fund............. | 26 |
| Coast Guard general gift fund................. | * |
| Deepwater port liability fund................. | 2 |
| Federal ship financing fund, revolving fund, Maritime Administration................ | 37 |
| Highway trust fund............................ | 8,749 |
| Offshore oil pollution compensation fund...... | 27 |
| War-risk insurance revolving fund, Maritime Administration...................... | $1 |
| **Department of the Treasury:** | |
| Exchange Stabilization Fund................... | 3,011 |
| Assessment fund............................... | 88 |
| Other......................................... | 1 |
| **Veterans Administration:** | |
| Veterans reopened insurance fund.............. | 487 |
| Veterans special life insurance fund.......... | 797 |
| National service life insurance fund.......... | 8,311 |
| Servicemen's group life insurance fund........ | 37 |
| United States Government life insurance fund.............................. | 356 |
| General post fund, national homes............. | 5 |

## FIGURE 44 (continued)

| | |
|---|---|
| Environmental Protection Agency: | |
| Hazardous substance response trust fund....... | 424 |
| Other independent agencies: | |
| Federal Deposit Insurance Corporation......... | * 13,334 |
| Federal Home Loan Bank Board: | |
| Federal Savings and Loan Insurance Corporation................................ | 5,159 |
| General Services Administration: | |
| National Archives trust fund................ | 3 |
| National Archives gift fund................. | * |
| Harry S Truman Scholarship Foundation......... | 40 |
| Japan-United States Friendship Commission................................ | 19 |
| National Credit Union Administration: | |
| National credit union share insurance fund.. | $200 |
| Office of Personnel Management: | |
| Civil service retirement and disability fund | 95,858 |
| Employees health benefits fund.............. | 664 |
| Employees life insurance fund............... | 4,680 |
| Retired employees health benefits fund...... | 1 |
| Railroad Retirement Board: | |
| Railroad retirement account................. | 1,190 |
| Railroad retirement supplemental account.... | 30 |
| Small Business Administration................ | 14 |
| United States Postal Service................. | 2,572 |
| Total held by Government accounts.......... | $216,405 |
| The public: | |
| Interest-bearing.............................. | $924,478 |
| Noninterest-bearing........................... | 1,151 |
| Total held by the public.................... | $925,629 |
| Total public debt securities................ | $1,142,034 |

"bonds", presumably to "insure" savings deposits. This gives you some idea of the legitimacy of the government's claim that it "insures" bank deposits.[11] In any case, the Committee admits that the initial premise upon which Social Security was based (the creation of a reserve based upon government bonds) was an illusion and the government now seeks to perpetuate Social Security by the creation of other illusions.

## Other Startling Committee Observations

Next note the Committee's astute observation that payment of Social Security taxes (Figure 41, [f]) ". . . has a very real affect on capital formation in this country . . .". This observation certainly took *a good deal of expertise!* Obviously a system that collected approximately $75 billion in 1974 (the year prior to the study) or approximately 30% of all Federal revenues, *must have* a "real effect" on capital formation since, if this $75 billion had not been forceably extracted from the private sector, a good portion of it could have gone into investments, i.e. capital formation. *Exactly* how much is not known, but obviously a substantial reduction in capital

[11] The government intends to make good on its "insurance" claims — not with the bonds it holds, but by the phony currency it may print to pay such claims. Such counterfeiting of currency doesn't meet these commitments, it means that the government will loot the deposits of some (through inflation) in order to meet its obligations to others. The value of such payments and deposits will, therefore, depend on how much money the government prints. As long as there are trees in Canada, the government can always print enough to "pay" its claims. Of course, this *money* "may not be worth anything when recipients get it" (see page 154), but this is obviously how Washington plans to "pay" its bills, *including FDIC commitments.*

formation must occur whenever the government takes that much money away from the public.

For comparison purposes it might be noted that the total amount invested by business and industry in new plant construction and equipment in 1974 was $157 billion, of which $20 billion was spent by public utilities. So if only 1/4 of what was collected in Social Security taxes in 1974 had been invested by the public, that would have been equal to the amount that all America's utility companies invested in new plant construction and equipment in 1974.

### *Social Security Taxes Now Take Far More Out Of The Economy Than Private Citizens Save*

Total private savings in 1974 were $85 billion. Social Security collections alone, therefore, amounted to approximately 90% of all private savings. However, by 1982, Social Security taxes of $200 billion exceeded private savings by 40%! This *must have* a substantial negative effect on capital formation, even if we don't know *precisely* how much, due to the fact that such taxes are transferred back to the public who could, in turn, save a portion of them.

Social Security taxes, remember, *are paid by producers* who might otherwise have saved a portion, while Social Security benefits *are paid to non-producers* who obviously use their checks for consumption purposes and not for savings.

There is, of course, no way to know exactly how much capital formation is destroyed by Social Security taxes, but precise figures are not important. What is obvious, however, is that Social Security taxes *must substantially reduce capital formation.* Savings in

America are now only 4½% of personal income — the lowest level in our history![12] Since capital is essential for jobs, it is obvious that the marked reduction of capital formation caused by Social Security has substantially reduced the number of jobs available in the private sector. So, when a Committee on finance observes that ". . . even with the current cost method, the OASI system has affected the capital formation of this country and will continue to affect it in ways *that are not clearly understood at this time. . .*", I must ask, "Not clearly understood by whom?" If members of that "finance" Committee did not "clearly" understand this simple issue then they had no right to be on it, or any other, "finance" committee for that matter.

### *Committee Recommends Another Committee!*

Note the Committee's recommendation that yet *another* committee study this problem. I outlined the same problem in 1976 — what further *study* is required? The only further study required is a *study* on how to dismantle the entire program so as to cause the least financial injury to those who (unfortunately) have come to rely on it.

The Committee also observed (Figure 42, [g]) that the weighting of Social Security benefits "represents society's recognition of 'adequacy' as a criterion of the plan and is a departure from the strict principle of individual equity"; that the ". . . Social Security pro-

[12] With the possible exception of a few years following World War II when savings dropped to extremely low levels as the nation went on a buying binge.

gram is necessarily a blend of social goals and individual equity"; and that "Maintaining the proper blend is very important if we are to sustain the workers' support of the plan". Just who determined the "adequacy" of the plan, the *blend* of "social *goals* and individual *equity"*, and what expertise did such people have to make such judgements? More importantly, where in the United States Constitution is the Federal government authorized to determine a necessary *blend* of "social goals and individual equity"; and just what does it mean?

The council further states (Figure 42, [h]) that in order to "sustain the worker's support" they have to "view their protection as being reasonably related to the taxes they pay". Since, at this point, Social Security benefits are not all related to current levels of taxation or to the prospect of even getting future benefits, the Committee euphamistically admits that workers must be tricked into "viewing their benefits as being reasonable" in order to "sustain (their) support". In other words, it isn't that the benefits *are* related to the taxes being paid, they only have to be *perceived* (by the suckers) as being related!

## The Joint Economics Committee of Congress — The Blind Leading The Blind

Turning back once again to the May 27th hearing before the Congressional Joint Economics Committee of Congress (before which Mr. Wallis made the remarks shown on page 131), the two day hearing was opened by the following statement of then Committee chairman, the late Senator Hubert Humphrey:

### Opening Statement of Chairman Humphrey

Chairman Humphrey. Mr. Cardwell, and your associates, thank you very much for your patience. We have a rather rugged day in the Senate today. I was on my way over to see you and all at once the bell rang and we returned to our first line of duty.

This morning, the Joint Economic Committee begins 2 days of hearings on the problems of the social security system. Of course the concern over the social security system is everywhere, and people are asking a number of questions about the solvency of the system and its continuity. We hope to discuss these problems in a clear, objective fashion and begin to determine the best course for Congress to pursue over the coming years. We want to assure the financial soundness of this crucial social insurance program. We know full well that this will not be an easy task. But there are numerous problems facing our social insurance system, and there is disagreement over the seriousness of some of these problems.

Note here that the government recognized that "concern over the Social Security system is everywhere, and people are asking a number of questions about the solvency of the system and its continuity". Well, the situation continued to get worse following these hearings which proves that all such hearings are a waste of taxpayer's money!

*Martin Feldstein's Remarks to the Committee*

Among the more interesting observations made that day to the Committee were those of Martin Feldstein who now serves as President Reagan's Chairman of the Council of Economic Advisors. He stated:

Although there has been much concern about the social security program's unfunded liability of more than $2 trillion, there is no economic reason why social security should ever be bankrupt. Current beneficiaries and covered workers are expected to receive over $2 trillion in benefits more than they are expected to pay in future taxes.

If social security were a private pension plan, it would require current assets of more than $2 trillion to be financially solvent, i.e., to guarantee its ability to meet its future obligations.

Since the social security program has a trust fund of only $44 billion or some 2 percent of its obligations, social security is bankrupt by the conventional standards used to determine the actuarial soundness of private pension programs.

This analogy of social security to private pension programs is, however, totally misleading. A private pension program must have sufficient assets that any future contributions will be made. In contrast, the Government can continue to compel future generations of workers to pay social security taxes. The future tax rates can be set so that tax revenues are sufficient to meet the claims of the beneficiaries.

The Government's power to tax is its power to meet the obligations of social security to future beneficiaries.

As long as the voters support the social security system, it will be able to pay the benefits that it promises. It is therefore very important to prevent an increase in the tax rate or other changes that will undermine public support of social security's primary purpose: Providing basic income-related annuities that individuals otherwise would not or could not buy for themselves. Maintaining political support will become even more difficult because of the problem to which I now turn.

There are, of course, a number of misconceptions in this short excerpt from Feldstein's lengthy testimony. First of all, he states that current beneficiaries and covered workers are expected to receive over "... $2 trillion in benefits more than they are expected to pay in future taxes". Please tell me, Mr. Feldstein, just *who is* going to pay the extra "$2 trillion" (in real purchasing power) more than was paid in? The taxpayers of France... or England ... or the Soviet Union?

How is this financial hat trick to be pulled off? How are Americans going to (collectively) take $2 trillion more out of a program than they (collectively) put into it — without any capital creation from which such payments will be generated? In case you're wondering,

Senator Proxmire (as will soon be shown) supplied the answer! But when Feldstein admits that Social Security would need more than $2 trillion to be currently solvent (four times as much as the then reported national debt), and that it only had 2% of its obligations,[13] he is obviously admitting that Social Security *even then* was way beyond salvaging! Note Feldstein's admission that ". . . Social Security is *bankrupt* by the conventional standards used to determine the actual soundness of private pension programs. . .". But that was the basis upon which the system was sold to the nation and the basis upon which it was held to be constitutional by the Supreme Court. And, if the plan is bankrupt by "conventional standards", then on what standards is it solvent? Feldstein's answer is that it is solvent because "the government can continue to compel future generations of workers to pay Social Security taxes". MR. FELDSTEIN, THIS BOOK PROVES YOU ARE WRONG AGAIN!!

*Proxmire's Answer to Feldstein's Riddle*

I now offer the pièce de resistance — proof that not only is Social Security a fraud that can wreak havoc on the nation — but that politicians cannot be trusted to administer this or any other financial program.

At these same hearings, Senator Proxmire was questioning James P. Cardwell, the Commissioner of Social Security, regarding the prospect of "default" which had been raised by Senator Percy. Senator Prox-

[13] By 1982 the OASI had 0% of its obligations and would need over $5 trillion to be "currently solvent", or *five times* the reported national debt!

mire noted that betweeen 32 and 34 million people were drawing Social Security benefits and then went on to add:

> "Almost all of them, or many of them, are voters. In my State, I figure there are 600,000 voters that recieve Social Security. Can you imagine a Senator or Congressman under those circumstances saying, we are going to repudiate that high a proportion of the electorate? No.
>
> Furthermore, we have the capacity under the Constitution, the Congress does, to coin money, as well as to regulate the value thereof. And therefore we have the power to provide that money. And we are going to do it. *It may not be worth anything when the recipient gets it,* but he is going to get his benefits paid." (emphasis added)

To which Commissioner Cardwell replied, "I tend to agree."

So here we have Senator Proxmire stating that while politicians might be reluctant (due to political considerations) to repudiate Social Security benefits honestly and openly, they would have no compunction about doing so underhandedly and surreptitiously — by the use of printing press money.

The apparent answer to Feldstein's riddle is that the printing press is expected to supply the extra $2 trillion! Now mind you, Senator Proxmire was head of the Senate Banking, Housing and Urban Affairs Committee. Somebody should have, therefore, explained to him what the consequences of Social Security checks being "not worth anything" would be. Maybe the good Senator didn't realize that if Social Security checks weren't "worth anything", neither are government bonds, savings accounts, and all other fixed dollar assets. What then would the social, economic and political climate of this country be if all currency and fixed dollar assets suddenly weren't "worth anything"?

Yet, note with what nonchalance Senator Proxmire (and, indeed, the entire Committee) accepted this unspeakable calamity. In addition, somebody should also have pointed out to Proxmire that "printing" money is not exactly the same as "coining" it, so he was slightly confused concerning the "capacity" he thought he and Congress had "under the Constitution".

Incidentally, Proxmire's statement and the manner in which it was accepted by the Joint "Economics" Committee, gives you some idea of the real intelligence level of The United States Congress and that of its committees.

## "Compact" Between Generations

Figure 45 is an excerpt from a current Social Security pamphlet. Note that the reader is informed that Social Security was "conceived as a *compact* between generations". Such a statement is a bold-faced lie.

No such "compact" was ever suggested or hinted at by those proposing Social Security, and it certainly was not in the minds of the public when it accepted Social Security. If a "compact" ever existed, how did earlier generations (who received generous Social Security benefits) discharge their "responsibility" under this "compact"? By agreeing to accept benefits out of all proportion to what they paid?

The government is obviously trying to con and intimidate younger Americans into believing that they are bound by some kind of "compact" under which *they* are (and will be) forced to deliver on the irresponsible

## FIGURE 45

Your parents, perhaps, are among those whose sense of dignity and independence is assured through monthly tax-free, inflation-proof checks, and whose health care needs are paid for, in part, by Medicare. Medicare helps relieve the families of older beneficiaries of potentially overwhelming financial responsibilities. !

Conceived as a compact between generations and between the people and their Government to meet the *basic* income needs of Americans, social security provides a financial foundation on which to build other savings for future income.

This commitment is a "pay-as-you-go" system, making a direct transfer of money from workers to those who are retired or disabled, and to the families of workers who are disabled or have died. Your benefits will be provided from the taxes of future workers. Today's taxes are used for today's needs. Ninety-eight cents of every social security tax dollar is paid out in benefits. Ha!

The strength of the social security system is that it is able to adjust to changing social patterns and economic conditions. It is reviewed constantly by Congress and the Administration and altered to adjust to changing conditions. Sufficient revenues are assured by examining economic projections and scheduling taxes which will raise enough revenues to cover the projections.

**U.S. Department of Health, Education, and Welfare,** Social Security Administration. HEW Publication No. (SSA) 79-10053, August 1979 promises made over the last 47 years by vote-seeking politicians. Older Americans foolishly believed that their benefits would come out of their own "contributions". Since, admittedly, these "contributions" are gone — voilà, we now have a "compact"!

## More Official Admissions

On November 3, 1976 an article written by the then Secretary of the Treasury, William Simon, appeared in *The Wall Street Journal* and opened as follows: (emphasis added)

> "As chief financial officer of the U.S. government, I am required to assess the soundness of the Social Security system. My assessment covers both the system's currently financial position, and its ongoing visibility. I have been shocked by what I have learned. Even though I am sure there is no immediate danger, the future prospects of the system as we know it are grim. . ."

Quoting further, he said:

> "What has gone wrong? And why is the problem expected to get so much worse in the future?
>
> Since 1935, when the Social Security Act became law, the government has tinkered with the program. Bit by bit the soundness of its financing has been undermined. It was originally understood, at least in the way the program was presented to the public, that the premiums contributed (Social Security tax payments) would be accumulated in a reserve account, just like the pension fund of a business firm or labor union. This fund was supposed to grow steadily, earning interest, until it reached an amount large enough to meet its commitments. The contributors themselves would own the assets in the fund, for which the government would

serve merely as trustee. The members' economic security in old age would be fully protected by this ownership. They would never have to depend on anyone else's charity for their livelihood."

## A Lifeline Needed

Today, Social Security actually operates in a very different fashion. The reserve account (later relabeled the Trust Fund) has not been allowed to grow to more than a fraction of the required size. Instead, the government has used much of the money contributed by wage earners to pay increased benefits to people whose contributions were not enough to warrant those benefits. The government has also failed to raise taxes commensurately with benefit increases. As a result, the Trust Fund is so meager that it is barely enough to keep the *program going* for six months . . ."

and:

"There is really nothing we can do about the insufficiency of the Trust Fund. It is far too late to rebuild it to the required size. For that an astonishing amount of money would be needed-by official estimates, more than two full years of our entire GNP! That is not practical, and it would not be desirable even if it were practical. Our past mistakes are behind us, and all we can do is to avoid repeating them in the future.

In any event, today's contributors have not been building a fund at all. The taxes they are paying into Social Security are being merely handed over as benefits to other people. In turn, when the current workers retire, they will be *completely dependent* upon future workers for their benefits. *Their position is even more vulnerable should anything go wrong with this delicate balance.* Each generation has the power through the elective process to refuse to pay.

> *If the next generation were to refuse to pay the retired population would be helpless. . ."*

and finally:

> ". . .To put the point bluntly. I can see no way in which the government's current *promises can be kept. For the problem is even worse than official projections suggest. . ."* (emphasis added throughout)

At the time this article was written Simon (as Secretary of the Treasury and Chief Trustee of the Social Security "trust fund") was in as good a position as anyone to accurately evaluate Social Security. His appraisal, of course, was entirely accurate when he stated that he could "see no way that the government promises could be kept". This admission, of course, branded those promises as irresponsible and fraudulent. Despite all this, however, Simon's article was not entirely forthright since he devoted the last quarter of it to suggesting possible ways the program could be salvaged. True, he suggested that such changes "will not be popular", but he also suggested that some changes might salvage the plan when it was obvious that it is not salvageable at all. Maybe it was too much to expect that the then Secretary of the Treasury could blow the whistle *completely*; but his remarks should have been enough to expose the program as one of the biggest political and bureaucratic scandals in history!

When Simon admitted that Social Security's problems were "even worse than official projections suggest", he was backing up Wallis' admission (see page 131) that the public's misunderstanding of Social Security was "deliberately cultivated" by the government. This deception continues to this very day.

The point is that all the material included in this chapter establishes beyond a doubt that Social Security (as it is currently operated) is not at all like the program originally presented to the nation in 1935 or that was held constitutional by the Supreme Court. As a matter of fact, based upon the government's own admissions, it is clear that Social Security (as currently operated) is *openly* and *admittedly* unconstitutional!

In addition, a plan that has funds to last only 12 days (after 47 years of operation), and that *admittedly* may be paid off with checks that "may not be worth anything", is obviously not a plan that can be counted on to save anyone from the "rigors of the poor house"; but may, itself, be the very instrument that insures that many will get there!!

## SUMMARIZING THE POINTS COVERED IN CHAPTER 7

1. The fact that there have been numerous government studies of Social Security as well as several standing committees (including a trustee's committee) charged with the responsibility of monitoring Social Security did not prevent the OASI account from being dead broke in 1982. This proves that it is foolish to believe in or rely on the Federal government for anything it says or does.
2. The government now openly admits that there is no Social Security "reserve" and Social Security payments are made on a pay-as-you-go basis (the same basis upon which a chain letter or Ponzi scheme operates).
3. All government "trust funds" composed of government bonds (allegedly to support various government-backed programs) are an illusion and can be

of no financial help in supporting those programs they allegedly back.

4. Government "guarantees" are backed by nothing more than the government's willingness to print money which, in the final analysis, wipes out the value of all that is "guaranteed".

# 8

# *Of Taxes And Trust Funds*

When the government argued the legality of Social Security in 1938 (as explained in Chapter 5), it maintained that Social Security taxes were to be received by the Treasury as regular tax collections and were *not earmarked for any purpose whatsoever.* Yet the Act itself provided for the creation of a "trust fund", supposedly to *guarantee* the benefits promised. Figure 46 is a reproduction of Title 2, Section 201 that theoretically established this "fund".

Not only did the public *believe* that Social Security was to be secured by a gigantic "reserve" (as explained in Chapter 6), but the law also provided for such a "reserve" and further provided that such a reserve was to be maintained on the basis of "accepted actuarial principles". The Supreme Court relied on this provision in the law when it held Social Security constitutional as the following excerpt from *Helvering vs. Davis* makes clear:

> "The first section of this title creates an account in the United States Treasury to be known as the Old-Age Reserve Account.' Para. 201. No present approp-

> riation, however, is made to that account. All that the statute does is to authorize appropriations annually thereafter beginning with the fiscal year which ends June 30, 1937. How large they shall be is not known in advance. The 'amount sufficient as an *annual premium*' to provide for the required payments is 'to be determined on a *reserve basis* in accordance with *accepted actuarial principles* and based upon such *tables of mortality* as the Secretary of the Treasury shall from time to time adopt, and upon an interest rate of 3 *per centum* per annum *compounded annually*.' Para. 201(a). Not a dollar goes into the Account by force of the challenged Act alone, unaided by acts to follow." (emphasis added)

Note that the constitutionality of Social Security was based upon the Court's belief that an actuarially sound "reserve" was to be created in order to pay the benefits established by the Act. See how the court accepted such actuarial terms as "annual premiums", "reserves", "actuarial principles", "tables of mortality", "investment yield", etc. Obviously the court thought it was dealing with a legitimate pension plan; but such terms are meaningless when applied to "Social Security". The Court, however, did not understand this and,

# FIGURE 46

## TITLE II—FEDERAL OLD-AGE BENEFITS

### OLD-AGE RESERVE ACCOUNT

SECTION 201. (a) There is hereby created an account in the Treasury of the United States to be known as the "Old-Age Reserve Account" hereinafter in this title called the "Account". There is hereby authorized to be appropriated to the Account for each fiscal year, beginning with the fiscal year ending June 30, 1937, an amount sufficient as an annual premium to provide for the payments required under this title, such amount to be determined on a reserve basis in accordance with accepted actuarial principles, and based upon such tables of mortality as the Secretary of the Treasury shall from time to time adopt, and upon an interest rate of 3 per centum per annum compounded annually. The Secretary of the Treasury shall submit annually to the Bureau of the Budget an estimate of the appropriations to be made to the Account.

(b) It shall be the duty of the Secretary of the Treasury to invest such portion of the amounts credited to the Account as is not, in his judgment, required to meet current withdrawals. Such investment may be made only in interest-bearing obligations of the United States or in obligations guaranteed as to both principal and interest by the United States. For such purpose such obligations may be acquired (1) on original issue at par, or (2) by purchase of outstanding obligations at the market price. The purposes for which obligations of the United States may be issued under the Second Liberty Bond Act, as amended, are hereby extended to authorize the issuance at par of special obligations exclusively to the Account. Such special obligations shall bear interest at the rate of 3 per centum per annum. Obligations other than such special obligations may be acquired for the Account only on such terms as to provide an investment yield of not less than 3 per centum per annum.

Ha! ←

(c) Any obligations acquired by the Account (except special obligations issued exclusively to the Account) may be sold at the market price, and such special obligations may be redeemed at par plus accrued interest.

(d) The interest on, and the proceeds from the sale or redemption of, any obligations held in the Account shall be credited to and form a part of the Account.

(e) All amounts credited to the Account shall be available for making payments required under this title.

(f) The Secretary of the Treasury shall include in his annual report the actuarial status of the Account.

in its ignorance, believed and relied on the *illusion* created by the law. In any case, the Supreme Court obviously believed that the government's ability to "save men and women from the rigors of the poor house" rested on the creation of a legitimate *financial reserve* similar to those maintained by insurance companies. Would the court have believed that individuals could be "saved" purely on the basis of a pay-as-you-go chain letter? This point is a key element in the Supreme Court's holding that Social Security was constitutional. It was the Court's belief (misguided though it was) that the payment of old-age benefits *was to be tied into the creation of a sound actuarial reserve.*

The government now openly admits that such a "reserve" doesn't exist and that Social Security is based solely on a pay-as-you-go basis. In addition, a government-appointed Finance Committee further admits that even if a "reserve" did exist, it would be of no benefit (see page 143)! The government *admits,* therefore, that the constitutionality of the current, pay-as-you-go Social Security system has never been established by *any* court, nor could it be!

## Other Court Misconceptions

In 1938 the Court also believed that the Federal government was in a strong financial position to take on these commitments[1]: "State and local governments,"

[1] The government was financially strong in 1935 but that certainly is not the case today. In 1935 the Federal government's total funded and unfunded liabilities amounted to approximately $20 billion. Today those liabilities are over $10 *trillion,* or 500 times greater! This is only part of the price that the American public must now pay for its collective folly in repeatedly sending drunken sailors to the U.S. Congress.

Cordoza pointed out, "are often lacking in the *resources* that are necessary to *finance* an adequate program of security for the aged". (emphasis added)

Apart from deciding how much is "adequate", it is obvious that the Court (in holding Social Security constitutional) again indicated its belief that old age benefits would be *financed* and paid for out of legitimate "resources" presumably acquired, invested, and maintained by the Federal government.

## Printing Press Money Is Not A "Resource"

Again, referring back to the hearing that took place on May 27, 1976 (before the Joint Economics Committee), W. Allen Wallis, Chairman of the Advisory Council on Social Security, explained the public's misconception of Social Security when he stated:

> "When you pay Social Security taxes you are in no way making provisions for your retirement. You are paying the pensions of those who already are retired. Once you understand this, you see whether you will get the benefits you are counting on when you retire depends on whether the Congress will levy enough taxes, borrow enough, *or print enough money,* and whether it will authorize the level of beneifits you are counting on." (emphasis added)

Wallis' reference to the government's (illegal) ability to "print enough money" was again reiterated by Senator Proxmire who noted that the government has "the power" (but obviously not the right) to deliver money that "may not be worth anything when the recipient gets it." (For the full quote, see page 154.)

It must be obvious that *printing press money* was

not exactly the type of "resources" the Supreme Court had in mind. Such "resources" were not even available to the Federal government when the Supreme Court rendered its decision. At that time Federal Reserve and U.S. Notes were domestically convertible into silver, while, internationally, the U.S. was on a gold exchange standard. If private citizens couldn't exchange their currency for gold, foreign central banks could (which *to some degree* helped to keep the Federal government honest). Now all U.S. currency is counterfeited (made to resemble coined money and redeemable notes).[2] These worthless paper "dollars" and "slugs" are not authorized to circulate as money by the U.S. Constitution. In fact, the writers of the Constitution included *specific provisions to bar* such criminal practices by both Federal and state governments.

If city and state governments could have printed their own "money" back in 1935 with the same impunity that the Federal government does today, then they, too, would not have lacked the "resources. . .necessary to finance (their own) adequate program of security for the aged". Once again we see that the Supreme Court's 1935 decision was based on assumptions that absolutely do not apply to Social Security as it operates today.[3]

[2] See Chapter 1, *The Biggest Con* — "The U.S. Money Swindle".

[3] So, not only does the Federal government operate the world's largest Ponzi scheme, it is also the world's biggest counterfeiter and, of course, collects U.S. income taxes through out-right extortion. In essence, the Federal government consists of a collection of embezzlers, counterfeiters and extortionists! And, what is even more ludicrous is that these are the same clowns who want us to give them $250 billion a year so that they can "protect" us from the Russians!

## Fundamental Illegality of Social Security Now Openly Admitted

As explained on page 94, the Supreme Court held Social Security constitutional because it refused to face the following issue: Were Social Security taxes earmarked for Social Security benefits (as argued by Davis), or were they general receipts designed to provide the government with ordinary revenues (as claimed by the government)? Now, some 47 years later, the Federal government itself has openly admitted and emphatically answered this question — Social Security taxes (regardless of how the "law" is worded) go to pay Social Security benefits — period!

Chapter 7 contains reference after reference wherein one government committee after another openly admits that Social Security taxes are used to pay for Social Security benefits. Even the captions that have now been inserted into the law itself proclaim that Social Security taxes go to pay for Social Security benefits! Let me quote again from Wallis' statement to the Joint Economics Committee:

> "Many people think that the Social Security taxes taken out of their wages and sent to Washington each month provide for their old age pensions and other social security benefits. This simply is not the case. *Those taxes are levied on workers in order to pay benefits to people who already have retired and are drawing their Social Security pensions or to pay other Social Security benefits to those who already are drawing them."*
> *(emphasis added)*

In the face of such testimony (and in the face of a mountain of evidence now available that was not available in 1937), can the Federal government now claim that Social Security taxes are *not levied for the purpose of paying Social Security benefits;* but, rather, are needed to pay the ordinary expenses of government?

## Social Security Taxes Admittedly Levied To Pay Social Security Benefits

Social Security taxes are routinely increased (even while regular taxes are *presumably* cut) based solely on the government's contention that increased Social Security taxes are needed to pay increasing Social Security costs. In the face of this, will the government dare contend (as it did in 1938) that Social Security taxes are *not* "earmarked" for Social Security purposes but, instead, are increased solely to meet the general expenses of the Federal government? Isn't it *obvious* (based on the [false] representation made by the government in the 1938 *Helvering* case) that the position then taken by the Court and the government's current admissions render Social Security openly unconstitutional? Can any objective, responsible and intelligent person claim otherwise? The unconstitutionality of Social Security on this one issue is an "open-and-shut" case. And, of course, the Act is blatantly unconstitutional on a variety of other grounds previously examined.

## 60% Of All Federal Expenditures Obviously Illegal

By allowing the Federal government to levy a "Social Security" tax for an obviously illegal purpose, the Supreme Court gave the government the green light to raise taxes for a variety of other (equally illegal) purposes. The very existence of Social Security served to confuse the American public as to whether or not the government could legally levy taxes to pay for anything it wanted.

American citizens are now compelled to work in order to pay taxes to bail out Mexican and Brazilian banks; to pay the interest on Polish bonds; to subsidize wheat for the Russian economy; to pay farmers not to grow food; to pay for college tuitions; to pay the rent of private citizens; to make loans to private businesses; and to bail out foreign economies — *all of which are illegal.* The Constitution, remember, only allows the Federal government to tax the American public for the following purposes:

1. To pay the debts of the United States — not to pay the debts of individuals, corporations or foreign countries.
2. To provide for the national defense — which means to provide for *our own* military forces and *perhaps* to help supply and equip military forces of a friendly power. This cannot, however, include economic aid. If this provision is stretched to include economic aid then the U.S. Constitution imposes *no* limitations on the governments capacity to spend money.
3. To provide for the general welfare of the United States. This *does not* mean to provide for the welfare of *specific* individuals or groups of individuals, corporations or foreign countries.

All of these expenditures are, of course, illegal; but what can the American public expect? It is obvious that Social Security is unconstitutional. What is *not* obvious is the number of other programs which are equally unconstitutional. A Supreme Court that would allow the Federal government to get away with Social Security will allow the Federal government to get away with anything!

## SUMMARIZING THE POINTS COVERED IN CHAPTER 8

1. The Social Security Act provided for a Social Security "reserve" to be maintained on the basis of "accepted actuarial principles".
2. In holding Social Security constitutional, the Supreme Court relied on the creation of such a "reserve" fund.
3. The government now admits that the fund (relied upon by the Supreme Court) does not exist, thus rendering the *Helvering* decision (predicated on such a "reserve") null and void.
4. The government's admitted willingness to pay Social Security benefits with (increasingly) worthless "paper money" was obviously not the type of financial "reserve" contemplated by the Court when it reviewed the Federal government's financial strength against that of local governments.
5. The open admission by the Federal government that Social Security taxes are used specifically to pay for Social Security benefits (exactly contrary to its claim before the Supreme Court in the *Helvering* case) establishes, without question, the unconstitutionality of Social Security.

# 9

# The System Encourages Rampant Abuse

In this treatise no attempt has been made to analyze the alleged benefits of Social Security or to attempt to show how similar benefits might be purchased cheaper through private insurance carriers since such considerations are, in my view, immaterial. If the Act is illegal (which it is), no other consideration is important. This book was designed to help people get out of the program and to provide them with the legal, moral and economic means to do so.

I could not, however, leave the subject of Social Security without exploring one other aspect of the program — its basic immorality. I believe that this area should be examined because advocates of Social Security always like to assume a superior moral attitude (as if those of us who oppose this swindle have no compassion for the elderly, the dependent or the disabled). These few examples taken from my own personal experience should illustrate that advocates of Social Security not only have no legal or economic basis for their beliefs, but they have no moral basis as well.

## Should Individuals Who Do Not Need or Want Social Security "Benefits" Be Compelled To

## Purchase Them?

In 1978 (while conducting a seminar in Los Angeles) a young lady stopped at the lectern and asked if I was going to explain "how to get out of Social Security". I told her that would depend on whether she was self-employed. If she were, I could help her get out of Social Security (as well as regular income taxes); but if she was working for someone else I probably could not. She said that she was self-employed and was, therefore, overjoyed at the prospect of being able to get out of Social Security. The woman seemed to be in her early thirties and explained that she had an incurable illness (the name of which I did not recognize then, nor can remember now). While I outwardly showed no emotion, I was actually extremely moved by her "matter of fact" disclosure that "I only have, at most, six more years to live". She apparently was unmarried and had no dependents and obviously had no expectation of living to retirement age. There would be, therefore, no benefit to anybody for the substantial Social Security taxes she was paying (forgetting the one-shot, lump sum death benefit of $255.00). She said she felt her Social Security taxes were a total waste of money since she didn't need to put aside money for her "retirement years" that she knew would never come. She wanted to be able to spend whatever money she earned to enjoy what time she had left.

For some reason she felt she had no need of any of the medical and/or disability benefits that Social Security also provided, but I didn't want to pry and, therefore, never found out why. The point is, that those do-good social planners who think they know how to organize everybody's lives forget about people with shortened life expectancies who are not at all concerned with "retirement". Should these people be compelled to participate in a retirement program that they have no need for and, in so doing, deny themselves things that they could otherwise enjoy? Why shouldn't people be free to spend *their own money* on the things *they* want? Is it because these liberal do-gooders believe that they know what's best for us, even if we don't?

## People Won't Save, So The Government Has To "Force" Them To Save

Over the many years that I have been arguing against Social Security, its advocates always argued that the reason we need Social Security is that "people just won't save for their old age and, therefore, the government has to *force* them to save". The implication of these arguments was always that Social Security *forced* people "to save". Such advocates argued that the government was taking Social Security taxes and putting them into a form of "savings plan" for such taxpayers. If this were really the case, Social Security might not have been such a bad idea. But the truth of the matter is that the government never "saved" one dime of what it took from the public in the form of Social Security taxes. The government simply took these taxes and spent them on a variety of government projects — many of which are totally insane (like paying farmers not to produce).

In essence, Social Security actually *prevented* the public from saving! True, not all the money paid into Social Security might have been saved, but if even a small portion of it had been, the capital wealth of this nation would be billions of dollars higher than it is today. In reality, not one penny of Social Security taxes was ever *saved* for anybody as the bleeding-heart advocates of it continually claimed.

## Social Security Disability Payments Breed Dependency

A friend of mine was a successful salesman in a specialized field but I never knew he only had one kidney until he had to have it removed. Shortly thereafter Steve spent a lot of time in the hospital attached to a dialysis machine. Eventually he was able to treat himself and he showed me the implants on his wrists which had to be attached to tubes on his home machine. Steve said that home dialysis wasn't really that bad — in fact, he could even have his treatments while watching television. In any case, he was surprisingly cheerful about the whole thing and optimistically looked forward to the day when he would again be able to earn the kind of money he had been used to. He was then, as I recall, receiving about $600-700.00 per month in Social Security disability payments; but that was what was causing his dilemma.

It seems that if he earned any money at all on his own he would lose his *entire* disability check. Government disability payments have to be issued strictly according to the law which apparently means either you are disabled or you are not — there is no provision in the law for subjective decision making.[1] A recent news article (see Figure 47) dramatically reveals

[1] This is probably as it should be, otherwise the law would not be administered uniformly and would, therefore, be subject to the whims and interpretations of bureaucrats. This is also precisely why the government shouldn't be in the disability business in the first place.

# FIGURE 47

The Dallas Morning News

Thursday, October 13, 1983

## 83-year-old woman may lose home, SS

*Associated Press*

HEMPSTEAD, Texas — An 83-year-old woman who is deaf and confined to a wheelchair may lose her home and Social Security income because of highway expansion near Hempstead.

Jessie Deslin lives in a house beside Texas Highway 6, which runs between Waco and Houston. The highway is scheduled to be widened from two lanes to four, and Mrs. Deslin's house is in the way of the expansion.

State highway officials offered to build a new house for Mrs. Deslin near her present one. They also offered Mrs. Deslin the option of moving her house 50 to 100 feet back from the highway.

Mrs. Deslin chose the second option and agreed to sell the highway department 1.25 acres of the 27 acres she owns near Hempstead. She was paid $9,718 for the land.

What Mrs. Deslin didn't realize was that moving the house would require that it undergo extensive improvements and repairs before she would be permitted to move back in. The move would cost her $3,000 to $5,000 that she doesn't have.

She also found out that Social Security officials now plan to curtail her $280-a-month Supplemental Security Income payment because of the money she received for her land.

Officials said the case is complicated because Mrs. Deslin is deaf, and they have had difficulty communicating with her. She often bursts into tears when discussing the situation.

Mrs. Deslin said the officials are "mean."

"I can't sleep at night because I'm so worried about what they're doing to me," Mrs. Deslin said. "I'm an old lady. Why are they being so mean to me? I just want to live out here in peace."

Michael Andreozzi, a Bellville, Texas, attorney representing Mrs. Deslin, said Social Security Administration rules forbid counting money received for relocations as income.

But Andreozzi said officials at the Social Security office in Brenham, Texas, refuse to change their minds concerning Mrs. Deslin's case.

Andreozzi said he has no choice but to take the case to court.

"They take her land, and they give her an amount of money that won't pay the cost of moving her house," Andreozzi said. "And, in the meantime, she loses her Social Security."

Highway department official Jim Pierce said he has tried to find a solution.

"She really didn't have any choice but to sell us that land," Pierce said. "We were going to get the property either way.

"I feel for the old lady, but there's only so much we can do. You can't communicate with her, and there's just nobody to take charge and made a decision for her. Every time I go out there, she cries."

Pierce said he has unsuccessfully battled the Social Security Administration in Mrs. Deslin's behalf.

this aspect of Social security. If Steve's benefits had been coming from a private charity or insurance company, such agencies would have worked out a program with Steve that might have allowed him to earn money so that he could gradually get back on his feet without cutting off his disability benefits completely. Such arrangements simply cannot be worked out (by law) with the government. Under such laws a person either accepts being disabled and gets all the aid he is eligible for or he tries to work and loses all those benefits. These government programs actually encourage citizens to become totally dependent and accept the government stipend rather than seek ways to become even partially self-supporting.[2]

## Foreign Freeloaders

Several years ago, while having lunch with two women of Italian extraction, the subject of taxes and Social Security came up. Anna, it turned out, was annoyed at the numbers of people she knew who apparently had come over from Italy just to qualify for Social Security. According to her, people came over from Italy and worked for five years or so and then went back to Italy and collected (by Italian standards) a sizeable retirement from *America's* Social Security program.

[2] Today there are provisions that would allow those who are disabled to earn money over a nine month period without losing benefits. But between the red tape, the arbitrary manner these provisions are enforced and the penalties involved for those who might attempt to work, recipients are, once again, encouraged to collect benefits for disabilities rather than try to become fully (or even *partially*) self-supporting.

Remember, Social Security is substantially weighted in favor of those who qualify for minimum benefits. Such individuals receive a much larger proportional benefit than those who pay higher taxes over a longer period of time. I was surprised by this disclosure since I had never heard of it before, so I asked, "How many people do you know who are actually doing this?"

"I know of at least ten people who are here from Italy for just that reason," Anna replied.

"Oh, come on Anna, you can't possibly know that many people who are here for that reason only," I said. Although New Haven, Connecticut has a substantial percentage of people who are of Italian extraction, I was still a little shocked by that figure and assumed that Anna was exaggerating a bit.

Even her friend Maria, while aware of the situation, agreed with me and turning to Anna said, "Come on Anna, you don't know *that* many."

Suddenly an animated discussion developed between the two as Anna attempted to prove her point.

"Well," said Anna, "there's Vinnie's uncle Fred; and how about Nicky's aunt Carmelina?" They continued talking, tallying up all those they knew who came from Italy to get on Social Security.

Finally, Maria turned to me and said, "Gee, Irwin, I guess we *do* know ten people who are here from Italy."

Needless to say, the revelation that these two women alone knew of at least ten people who had come here from Europe to rip-off the American taxpayer through the Social Security system shocked me.

While in Chicago I told that story to some people as we were eating dinner. One woman of Polish extraction said, "Well, they come over here from Poland for the same reason."

Apparently this is common and a well known fact in areas populated by large ethnic groups. Figure 48 is part of an IRS brochure, especially designed for people collecting Social Security benefits who live outside the United States. Note that the brochure comes printed in a variety of foreign languages. Obviously a number of these recipients didn't stay in America long enough to even learn our language! Note that the pamphlet instructs these foreigners that they should notify the U.S. government if their economic situation changes (so their benefits could be reduced accordingly). Can you see how American taxpayers are being ripped off? Do you think that such foreign nationals, living in a foreign country (receiving old age, disability or dependent benefits derived from working Americans), would be stupid enough to notify our government so that those benefits could be *reduced?* Especially when our government would have no way of knowing if or when such benefits should be reduced?! How stupid can the American public be?

### *The Unemployment Rip-Off*

While this book focuses especially on the OASDI aspect of Social Security, another part of the Act was the creation of unemployment "insurance". Though I can sympathize with the good intentions of those who favored such an "insurance" scheme, I am also well aware of the validity of the adage "the road to hell is paved with good intentions". I can think of no better proof of that wise saying than unemployment "insurance".

First of all, unemployment "insurance" is not *in-*

**FIGURE 48**

**Introduction**

This booklet explains how being outside of the U.S. may affect your Social Security checks. It also tells you what you need to report to us so we can make sure you receive all the Social Security checks you are entitled to receive. The information on pages 3-4 tells where to report and what to include in your report.

<u>This publication is also printed in Chinese, Croatian, Danish, Filipino, French, German, Greek, Italian, Japanese, Norwegian, Polish, Portugese, Serbian, Slovak, and Spanish.</u>

**When are you outside of the U.S.?**

When we say you are outside of the U.S., we mean that you are NOT in one of the 50 States, the District of Columbia, Puerto Rico, the U.S. Virgin Islands, Guam, or American Samoa. Once you have been away from the U.S. for at least 30 days in a row, you are considered to be outside the country until you return and stay in the U.S. for at least 30 days in a row.

**Want more information?**

If you want more information than this booklet gives or if you have any questions about Social Security, ask at any U.S. Embassy or Consulate or write to us at the address shown under "How to report" on page 3.

**Figure 48** (continued)

Things that must be reported

| page | |
|---|---|
| 5 | Change of address |
| 6 | Work outside the U.S. |
| 9 | Disabled person can work again or disability improves |
| 9 | Marriage |
| 10 | Divorce or annulment |
| 10 | Adoption of a child |
| 10 | Child leaves the care of a wife, husband, widow, or widower |
| 11 | Child nearing 18 is a full-time student or is disabled |
| 12 | Death |
| 13 | Inability to manage funds |
| 13 | Imprisonment for conviction of a felony |
| 14 | Deportation |

**U.S. Department of**
**Health and Human Services**
Social Security Administration
SSA Publication No. 05-10137
June 1983
**☆U.S. G.P.P. 1983- 381-551/ 12**

*surance* by any stretch of the imagination. From a purely economic point of view, such a program must *increase* unemployment.[3] Though it is not my purpose

[3] For an explanation, see *The Biggest Con,* pages 222–223.

here to examine the economic implications of this program, I would like, at least, to discuss how the program operates in the real world.

Several years ago I moved into an apartment complex in southern Florida. At the same time, another gentleman (who had operated his own real estate business in a northern city) moved in also. Since he was eligible for maximum unemployment compensation, he was determined not to begin work again until he had exhausted all his benefits — and he did just that. He relaxed by the pool and played tennis every day for a year, when he could easily have found employment had he had any incentive to do so. But why should he? He was getting a sizeable unemployment check so he could take a year-long vacation. He did go to the unemployment office each week and said that he was looking for, but could not find, a job. That, of course, was sheer bunk.

If the government had not been paying him *not* to work he would have found a job in short order. Everyone knows of similar instances where those collecting unemployment "insurance" really do not seriously bother to look for work until their benefits have run out.

### *Auto Workers – Getting More Money While Unemployed*

Many unemployed auto workers were actually receiving more money when they were laid off than they earned while working! Because of the bargaining power of the UAW, its members had a contract which provided that the automobile companies had to supplement state unemployment benefits, resulting in the auto workers receiving unemployment checks equaling approximately 90% of their working salary. The Federal government, however, had also inaugurated a program whereby those who became unemployed because of foreign imports would have their state benefits supplemented by an additional 40% in Federal money. In many cases, the combination of all these programs provided auto workers with more money while they were unemployed than they were getting while working!

*Hire and Fire Yourself!*

I once met an accountant who specialized in doing books for small taverns, bars and grills. He explained to me how many of these owners would put fictitious people on their payroll so that they, themselves, could collect unemployment benefits. After paying such a tax for six months or so, the owner would go down to the unemployment office and apply for benefits claiming he was the phantom worker who had been fired from the establishment. Should the agency check with the place of business, the owner, of course, would verify that the worker (himself) had, indeed, been fired. This scheme may have necessitated the creation of phony Social Security and identity cards, but the people involved in such schemes knew all these tricks. I discovered it was not all that difficult to fool bureaucrats with such shenanigans.

I also understand that many marginal production shops are run on the basis that those hired will work for five or six months and then be "fired" so they can collect unemployment benefits for six months to a year. There are lots of people who are apparently willing to work on this basis because they know they will be able to take a long, paid vacation after working for only a few months.

*Unemployed Actors and Ballplayers*

The whole country was alerted some months ago to the fact that Ronald Reagan's son would be collecting unemployment "insurance" between dancing engagements. This, again, is but another aspect of the unemployment "insurance" rip-off. In certain professions unemployment was always accepted as a matter of course. Actors were always "unemployed" between shows; entertainers and musicians were "unemployed" between engagements; baseball players generally did not work in the winter months; and hockey players were "laid off" in the spring and summer.

All such professions generally pay higher wages to compensate for these periods of "unemployment" between jobs and/or seasons. The system has now, however, introduced an entirely unnecessary and ludicrous element to occupations where "unemployment" had no real meaning and was inherent in the profession itself.

So who actually pays the cost of real estate brokers who take a year's vacation to swim and play tennis; or the small businessman who fires himself so he can collect; or entertainers who collect unemployment benefits between engagements; or individuals who work six months then get fired, taking a six month vacation every year? Who pays? *The public pays* in terms of higher prices for everything that they buy which inevitably leads to a lower standard of living. All Americans suffer a reduced standard of living because of the economic abuses created by unemployment "insurance"; which, in turn, was created by politicians who continually use the program to get votes from an uninformed and gullible public.

## Social Security Is In Trouble Because Americans Now Live Longer Than When The Program Was Established

While listening to the radio a few months ago, I heard a government official discussing the reasons he believed Social Security was in trouble. All the reasons he gave, of course, were sheer nonsense, but his major contention was that Americans were living far longer today than they were when the program was first established and, therefore, the program was in trouble.

What this bureaucrat *didn't* tell the public was that over the years Social Security has consistently employed no less than 25 actuaries. Why didn't these actuaries take into consideration the increasing life expectancy of Americans so that taxes and benefits could be adjusted accordingly? Can you imagine what would happen if John Hancock, Prudential, Metropolitan (or any other of America's insurance companies) sent out letters to those who purchased retirement policies years ago, stating that because Americans were currently living longer they could not give them the benefits promised in their policies? Congress would immediately launch an investigation and, if such were true, the officials of the company would be indicted and imprisoned. Well, the same thing should be done to government employees who promised certain "insurance" benefits to the American public and now are apparently welching on those promises.

## Social Security "Trustees" — Why Aren't They Liable?

Every year the trustees of Social Security (the Secretaries of the Treasury, Labor and HEW) issue a Trustee Report. Over the last dozen or so years each of these reports recommended substantial increases in Social Security taxes. Congress, however, (for obvious political reasons) never adopted the increases recommended by the trustees. The point is, what purpose did these "trustees" serve? The existence of trustees created the illusion that somehow "trustees" were watching the store. Normally, trustees have a fiduciary responsibility to protect the assets over which they have agreed to serve as trustees.

In the private sector, if there are trustees and it is discovered that the funds for which they have accepted responsibility are gone, the trustees are held *personally* liable. I don't see why Social Security trustees should be treated any differently since they agreed to be trustees in the first place. If they assume no personal liability, why were they called "trustees"? Were they called "trustees" merely to provide the public with a false sense of security?

In the past when trustees recommended substantial increases in Social Security taxes and Congress didn't go along with these recommendations, these trustees should have *resigned.* Such resignations would have alerted the American public that the program was in trouble. Instead, they made recommendations that were ignored and did absolutely nothing. These "trustees", therefore, aided and abetted Congress in creating the illusion that Social Security was sound and had the capital to pay for the benefits the government was promising. As such, these trustees are culpable and, in my view, *individually liable* for the fact that Social Security is now bankrupt and cannot pay the benefits promised. To the extent that such "trustees" are provided with pensions by the Federal government, such pensions should be stripped from them since there is no question that there is a debt they owe the American public. They *allowed* themselves to be used to mislead the nation.

## Government Officials Should Have Pensions Cut Before The Public Accepts Cuts In Social Security Benefits

In addition, the public should *demand* that elected officials (especially former members of Congress and members of the Presidential office) should have their generous government pensions cut before the public accepts any cuts in promised Social Security benefits. Why should the politicians who promoted the Social Security swindle be permitted to cut the public's pensions while receiving no cuts *in their own pensions?* I cannot see why past Presidents such as Nixon, Ford and Carter (who were minding the store when the American public was being swindled and lied to about Social Security) should now receive pensions and other benefits in excess of $100,000 per year — *each*!

In the event that it is claimed that government employees pay for their own pensions (as opposed to contributing to Social Security), all government employees should have their retirement pensions cut to the extent that the public must now accept cuts in Social Security benefits.

## SUMMARIZING THE POINTS COVERED IN CHAPTER 9

1. The payment of Social Security taxes compels many (those with shortened life expectancies and no dependents) to purchase "benefits" for which they have no need; denying them the right to buy, acquire and enjoy those things which are far more important to them.
2. While disability payments may appear to be humanitarian, they also promote dependency and discourage a return to some sort of productive work.
3. Social Security permits aliens to rip off the American taxpayer.
4. Unemployment "insurance" (a facet of the Social Security Act) is not insurance at all and, since it encourages rampant abuse, substantially lowers the nation's standard of living.
5. Social Security's so-called "trustees" should be held liable for the funds they oversee just as private trustees are responsible for the funds they oversee.
6. Government officials and employees should have their pensions cut (at last!) to the same extent that Social Security recipients have theirs cut.

# 10

## Why Dropping Out of Social Security Is In The National Interest

Social Security taxes paid by the employer and employee will be increased in 1984 to 13.7% of payroll (and to 14% in 1985) while Social Security taxes for the self-employed will jump from 9.35% to 11.3%. Thus self-employeds who earn $37,800 or more will find their Social Security taxes going up by $932.45 in 1984. A hard working, single entrepreneur (earning $37,800 from his own business) could find himself paying $4,271.40[1] in Social Security taxes *in addition to* a possible $8,000 in regular "income" taxes. His combined total Federal tax bill (forgetting about other Federal excise or state and city taxes) could be in excess

[1] The combined tax for employees receiving this amount in wages will be $5,178.60. Remember, though, that the *maximum* projected combined tax when Social Security started was *$180.00!*

of $12,000 leaving him with less than $25,000 to both live on *and* attempt to expand his business![2]

Given this level of taxation, is there anyone in his right mind who would claim that such an individual (and millions of others like him) is "free"? If they could, how do they then define serfdom? Or slavery?

It is obvious that working Americans are held in feudal bondage by a Washington bureaucracy that takes more from them than the 25% that medieval Lords extracted from their own serfs. What amazes me is why (supposedly) *free* Americans passively turn over so much of their productivity to government!

## Big Business Serves Big Government

Big business in America is not run for the benefit of the owners (the stockholders), but is run principally for the benefit of the Federal government[3] and the corporate employees (both blue collar and executive). The executives who run America's large corporations do not own these businesses and could resign or be fired tomorrow. They are, therefore, not going to stick their necks out (risking their positions) to implement a radical program that doesn't promise to significantly increase their own paychecks. They *refuse* to "rock the boat". Besides, they get enough non-taxable benefits (such as generous expense accounts, pensions and numerous other "perks") to take the sting out of the taxes they do pay. In addition, large corporations do a lot of business with the Federal government and so the

[2] The Federal government has practically guaranteed that the only way many small businesses can grow is if their owners perjure themselves on their tax returns in order to retain some of the money the government tries to extort from them.

[3] All of America's major corporations have actually been nationalized. See *The Biggest Con,* pages 137–139.

executives of these companies may be reluctant to jeopardize this relationship (a relationship they feel is dependent upon their willingness to collect taxes) as illegal as it might be.

Small businessmen,[4] on the other hand, won't be intimidated by such considerations. They are painfully aware of how taxes and never-ending red tape are undermining their businesses and, in turn, their ability to pass their businesses on to their children. It is the small businessman whose economic fortunes will *instantly* brighten by his refusal to go along with either paying or collecting Social Security taxes. For small businessmen, not paying *or* collecting these taxes may be the difference between staying in business or shutting down. By not withholding Social Security taxes from workers, employee wages will effectively be increased at no additional cost to the employer. In addition, the employer's portion can also be used to either increase capital or to further increase employee wages. It is my belief, therefore, that the small businessman will be instrumental in implementing the measures recommended in this book.

### *Social Security Taxes Responsible For Business Shutdowns*

Many large corporations would also benefit if they refused to go along with the Federal government's illegal taxing measures. The absentee ownership nature of corporate America (and its reliance on legal counsel[5]) simply prevents major American corporations from

[4] And there are 12,000,000 small businessmen and women in America today.

[5] Which guarantees that they will get the wrong legal advice with respect to Federal taxation.

acting in the best (long-term) interest of their stockholders. Perhaps stockholder suits should be instituted to stop America's large corporations from acting as government tax collectors to the detriment of both the corporations and themselves.

For example, Frank Bormann (President of Eastern Airlines) announced that unless Eastern employees took a 15% pay cut, Eastern would be forced into bankruptcy. The public is generally unaware that salary levels in America are *forced up* to compensate for the Federal taxes that are taken out. In addition, Federal taxes, in an economic sense, can be viewed as a Federal tax on payroll. In other words, an employee's *net* wage can be viewed as his *actual* wage, and all Social Security and withholding taxes that he and his employer pay can be viewed as a *single* excise tax paid by employers on their overall *net* payroll. You can see that on this basis alone Social Security taxes, plus the cost of their collection, easily accounts for 15% of employee payroll in the United States.

Since this is precisely the amount that Eastern said it needed to save in order to forestall bankruptcy, it is obvious that if their workers did not agree to a pay cut Eastern would have been forced into bankruptcy because of the cost of the Social Security taxes that the company believes it *has to* collect and remit to the Federal government. Because of such taxes Continental Airlines did, indeed, go bankrupt. If it could have avoided this expense (equivalent to 15% of its payroll), would it have gone out of business?

The same can be said of Braniff and Woolco. Would these two companies have gone out of business (creating economic and social *insecurity* for their employees) if they hadn't been subjected to such *unnecessary* and *artificial,* government-created payroll expenses?[6]

*Government Increases Payroll Costs 35%*

But wait, additional employee withholding taxes account for approximately another 20% of payroll which means that American businesses pay the Federal government a tax equivalent to about 35% of their payroll (apart from *all* the other taxes they pay) simply for the *privilege of staying in business!* Isn't it obvious that these artificial and unnecessary costs are the forces that are driving American companies (like Eastern, Continental, Braniff and Woolco) into bankruptcy? If Continental, Braniff and Woolco did not have these costs to contend with, would they have gone out of business or would Eastern have contemplated bankruptcy?

Prior to 1942, American businesses did not have to contend with such outrageous, artificial costs. They merely concentrated on turning out competitive products while generating and *retaining* the capital necessary to do it. Today, businessmen waste considerable time and energy merely trying to figure out ways to *avoid* paying taxes. A huge business in tax shelters has developed wherein a lot of human energy and time, as well as capital, is diverted into creating and searching for investments whose only merit is that they will generate tax deductions greater than the capital invested in them. Such wasteful investment activities were not a part of the American economic scene prior to 1942. No wonder America has lost its position as the

[6] Used mostly to fund illegal and asinine Federal projects.

world leader in the production of well-made, low-cost consumer goods.

Show me a businessman who might be contemplating going out of business, who would still consider doing so, if he understood that he was not required to pay either Social Security or ordinary "income" taxes. Not only would such an individual *not* consider going out of business, he would undoubtedly make plans to expand!

The social(ist) planners who promised American workers that Social Security would deliver all kinds of free goodies forgot to tell them that these goodies would be purchased by adding artifical costs to the price of *all* American-made goods; or that these very costs would (literally) collapse American businesses and spread the very economic and social *insecurity* that the program (Social Security) promised to eliminate. This is why the system should (correctly) be called Social *in*Security because that is what the program delivers.

## What Will Happen To The Country If Social *in*Security Is Eliminated?

First of all, true "social security" rests upon *economic* security which involves a society's ability to efficiently turn out a profusion of goods and services;[7] and it is obvious that Social *in*Security taxes substantially reduce America's ability to do just that! In the final

[7] A good example of this is Japan. One hundred million people with practically no resources have created a standard of living comparable to ours and actually outproduce us in many areas. True, we spend a greater percentage of our GNP than Japan does on national defense, but this hardly accounts for the difference. It wasn't too long ago that Japanese products simply couldn't hold a candle to American-produced goods. The question that Americans must ask is how can Japan do so much with so little while (in comparison) America now does so little with so much?!

analysis, it is not a question of whether Social *in*Security *will* end — the only question is *how* and *when* it will end. The recommendations of the 1983 President's Commission (to reduce Social *in*Security benefits by subjecting a portion to taxation and postponing retirement benefits for younger workers) amounts to an attempt to keep Social *in*Security alive by extracting higher taxes while giving even fewer benefits to Americans under 40. Unfortunately, these recommendations are only illusions used to postpone the day of reckoning. The Commission's projected Social *in*Security receipts did not take into account the destructive economic impact that higher Social *in*Security taxes (and higher budget deficits) must inevitably deliver.

## Irresponsible Politicians Will Allow Situation To Deteriorate

This nation is now too broke to send paychecks to 36 million people each month for *not working* and the U.S. Congress knows it. But that collection of overpaid, overpensioned influence-peddlars don't have the integrity or the backbone to honestly admit this to the public. They, therefore, will let matters get progressively worse (as long as they can continue to get reelected) until the roof caves in.

Congress knows that the 1983 deficit (as well as the projected deficits for the next several years) is in the neighborhood of $200 billion. Financing such deficits (at 10% interest) will add approximately $20 billion a year (in interest) to each succeeding year's budget. To put this sum in perspective, you need only consider that the total 1984 annual budgets for the Department of the Interior, the Department of Justice, the Department of State, the Department of the Treasury *and* the Environmental Protection Agency don't (collectively) amount to $18 billion a year! Therefore, Congress' unwillingness to balance the current year's budget (by cutting out expenditures that the nation obviously can't afford), means that *it is willing to add* the equivalent of *five* new departments and agencies to each succeeding year's budget! So, while the Federal government obviously cannot even afford *this year's* expenditures, Congress, nevertheless, intends to substantially *increase* next year's (and succeeding year's) expenditures!

### *How Congress Plans To "Deal" With The Problem*

Where will it all end? Senator Proxmire already gave us the answer: the government will eventually pay off Social *in*Security claims (and all other claims) with printing press money — *money that won't buy anything*! America's politicians are planning to duplicate here what happend in Germany in 1922. Such a situation will obviously create economic devastation comparable to an atomic attack and the destruction *will not* be wrought by Soviet missiles or foreign agents but, rather, by our own Congress! None of America's enemies ever succeeded in delivering the type of economic destruction that the U.S. Congress is planning for all of us if we don't stop them first.

Social *in*Security beneficiaries must understand that they have a vital stake in a healthy American economy. If the program that they think they need succeeds in collapsing that economy, where will they be? It is those Americans who are the *most* dependent who stand to suffer the most from the devastation that the U.S. Congress promises to deliver. Whether they realize it or not, it is Social *in*Security's present beneficiaries who most need to be saved from the dangers inherent in their own misguided hopes and beliefs.

## Do Federal Politicians Really Care About The Public?

Many people have been conned into thinking that Social *in*Security is a reflection of the Federal government's concern for the public. Such a belief is utter nonsense. Social *in*Security was created for no other reason than to allow vote-seeking politicians to get elected by promising gullible voters "something for nothing". As proof that Washington politicians do not give a hoot for the public, one need only consider the Federal government's agricultural policy. Its entire agricultural program is designed to do nothing but create food shortages in order to artificially drive up food prices.[8] If farmers ever organized (on their own) to do this they would end up in jail for violating the Sherman antitrust laws. It is amusing to consider that in Russia the government had to decollectivize a segment of its agriculture in order to increase food production, while in America the government, in essence, collectivizes agriculture in order to reduce production.

If the Federal government was really concerned about the public, would it force higher food prices on us? In 1983 the Federal government actually spent $19.4 billion ($2 million every hour!) buying up such food products as milk, butter, cheese, peanuts and wheat *just to keep them off the market!* In addition, taxpayers are charged hundreds of thousands of dollars a day just to store the stuff. The American taxpayer is, therefore, delivered a two-fold blow by the government's agricultural policies: he is *first taxed* in order to subsidize the program and he is *taxed again* in the form of having

[8] And the program is not even helping the farmers because other government economic and fiscal policies are artificially increasing farm costs for labor, interest and energy which are responsible for forcing farmers out of business.

to pay higher food prices because of the program! Is this the activity of a benevolent, considerate and rational government?

On November 7, 1983 *The New York Times* carried a front page story subtitled "House to vote on Measure to Pay Farms Not to Produce". It reported on a pending bill in the House of Representatives which, for the first time, "would pay dairy farmers to reduce production. . .".[9] Incredibly, in the same issue (page 20), there was another story captioned "Hunger Comes to Family's Table at Month's End". The article dealt with poverty in West Virginia and stated:

> "Like countless others who live in poverty across the country, the three children of Jerry and Betty Elkins know all too well what it is like to sit down to meager meals. 'We usually have bread and gravy the last few days of the month,' Mr. Elkins, who is 27 years old, said while waiting for a handout of Federal surplus food at Guyan Valley High School. 'This cheese and butter will really come in handy at our house.'
>
> The Elkinses glanced at their children, ages 5, 6 and 7, as they talked about trying to stave off hunger in one of the most economically depressed areas of the country."

The article went on to quote Mrs. Elkins as stating:

> "I couldn't tell you how many times we've made a meal on bread and water gravy, . . . The kids don't complain, though, and I tell them, 'At least we're not starving.' "

[9] This bill passed the House of Representatives (by a vote of 325 to 91) on November 9, 1983.

The article went on to report that:

> "Nancy Amedei, the director of the Food Research Action Center in Washington, D. C. has heard many such accounts. She says the country is teeming with hungry children."

It also said that Paul Smith of the Children's Defense Fund agreed with Ms. Amedei that hunger had become endemic among poor children in the United States and quoted him as saying:

> "We're not talking about acute, caloric starvation . . . This is not Bangladesh. What we're talking about is a regular and chronic lack of proper nutrition."

The article further stated that:

> "In McDowell County, where more than 30 percent of the work force is unemployed, school officials say hunger is a way of life for many children."

It also quoted Frances Whitten, the administrator of the county's school breakfast and lunch programs as stating:

> "Very definitely, there are hungry children in this county."

*Federal Government Creates "Poverty"*

So, while the nation is "teeming with hungry children" our representatives in Washington devise methods to cut food production! *What sort of idiotic nation have we become?!*

If it were not for the Federal government's policy of creating food shortages in order to drive up food prices, food would be so plentiful (and cheap) that the concept of poverty (associated with the inability to feed oneself) would be *unkown* in America. So if we *do* have poverty in our country it is because the morons in the U.S. Congress have created it!

By eliminating a number of government projects along with Social *in*Security (such as farm subsidies and minimum wage laws), we will eliminate *both* poverty and unemployment in one fell swoop and all Americans (including those currently on Social *in*-Security) will be a lot better off.

If, after eliminating such programs, any American still needed financial assistance, the additional prosperity that the elimination of these programs would create will allow local governments and private charities to help such individuals on a far better basis than they are how being "helped" by the Federal government.

In essence, those who cling to a belief in Social *in*Security (whether they know it or not) actually cling to a belief in socialism — the belief that centralized planning by bureaucrats can overcome economic need better than a free economy can. It should be pointed out that America developed into a powerful country *without* Social *in*Security and if such a program was unnecessary *before* 1942, it certainly is even less necessary today given all the advances in technology that have occurred since then.

## Most Government Expenditures Are Either Illegal Or Unnecessary

Figure 49 shows how the Federal government's 1984 revenues and expenses are allocated. Notice that direct payments to individuals account for 42% while grants to states and local communites account for another 11%, or a combined total of 53% of the total

## FIGURE 49

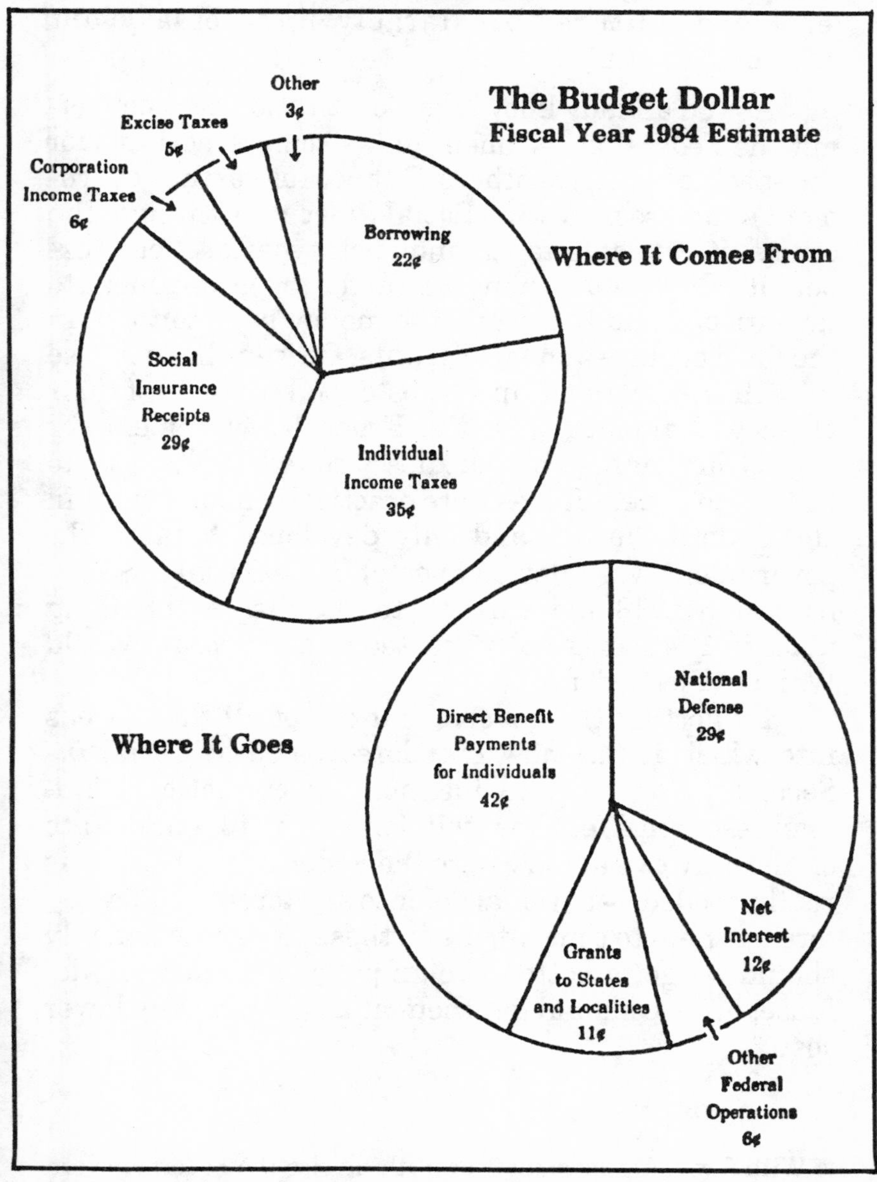
The Budget Dollar
Fiscal Year 1984 Estimate
Where It Comes From
Other
3¢
Excise Taxes
5¢
Corporation
Income Taxes
6¢
Borrowing
22¢
Social
Insurance
Receipts
29¢
Individual
Income Taxes
35¢
Where It Goes
Direct Benefit
Payments
for Individuals
42¢
National
Defense
29¢
Net
Interest
12¢
Grants
to States
and Localities
11¢
Other
Federal
Operations
6¢

Federal budget! This shows us that 53% of Federal expenditures are largely unnecessary *and* unconstitutional.

As you already know, the Constitution does not permit the Federal government to tax some Americans for the specific benefit of others. But because of the government's success in getting Social *in*Security through the courts, it was able to expand such types of illegal expenditures. It is also nonsensical for the government to tax citizens and then send the money back to them in the form of state and local grants. Citizens have to lose in such transactions since substantial portions of their taxes will remain with the Federal government for merely arranging this needless "round trip". Prior to 1942 such expenditures were practically nonexistant in the Federal budget and only developed because the government was allowed to establish a Social *in*Security tax in 1938 and, further, to establish withholding taxes in 1942 (originally created as a *temporary* World War II "Victory" tax).

By getting the government out of all those areas into which it has now blundered (such as Social *in*-Security, agriculture, education, labor relations, "human resources", etc.), we will force them to concentrate on the only two areas where the Federal government is really needed — national defense and foreign policy. By forcing them to concentrate in these two areas not only should we get a better foreign policy and national defense, but we should get them at a substantially lower cost.[10]

[10] With few exceptions, most everything else the Federal government does outside of these two areas should be left to either state or local governments, private enterprise, charitable organizations — or should not be done at all!

## Congress Will Not Act Responsibly — So You Must!

The Federal government is now so huge and unwieldy that it is impossible for it to control its own costs.[11] Government waste is rampant in one department after another. The continual increases in government expenditures have undermined and now threaten the nation's entire industrial plant. It must be recognized that America's military potential rests on its industrial base. Anything that undermines and weakens that base weakens America's military strength. Less taxation, therefore, is *essential* in order to improve America's industrial strength as well as its military power.

Federal politicians, however, now facing a $200 billion deficit, threaten to raise taxes *even further* in order to "reduce the deficit". There is no way (compatible with economic health) that taxes can be raised higher then they already are. If anything, they must be lowered!! But the only way that this can be done is if the U.S. Congress drastically reduces Federal spending. But an irresponsible Congress (fearful of losing the money and political support of various and sundry pressure groups) *will not* significantly cut Federal expenditures.

### *A Ticking Time Bomb*

Congress knows that a $200 billion deficit [12] is a ticking time bomb, but the scoundrels in Congress will

[11] The Federal government even now refers to better than 50% of its expenditures as "uncontrollable".

[12] Reported deficits below $200 billion will probably be inaccurate since they will not include "off budget" items. These unreported expenditures would have revealed that the 1982 deficit was actually $127 billion (which includes $17 billion in off budget items) and not the $110 billion reported.

do nothing to defuse it. They will be perfectly willing to sell out the nation's long-term welfare to gain their own immediate political ends.

Another major item in the Federal budget is interest. The American public now pays substantial amounts in interest on all the money that the Federal government borrowed to waste! It is important to recognize (in order to grasp the *full extent* of the U.S. Congress' total irresponsibility) that Congress has allowed a situation to develop wherein the interest now being paid by U.S. taxpayers on the Federal debt is *twice as great* as the taxes required to run all the other departments of government — with the exception of defense! Compare this to a family that spends twice as much on interest as it does on food. Would the manager of such a household be considered responsible? Well, these are the types of "managers" the public has been sending to Washington!

Though the government only needs about 35% of what it currently spends to cover its legitimate needs, even this is too high as I will explain. But, in any case, the government could easily collect this amount in excise taxes alone from the healthy economy that would be created if we would only eliminate 60% of what the Federal government does.

## Examples Of Government Waste

While national defense makes up 29% of the budget, there is no doubt that this includes a substantial amount of pure waste. For example, at a hearing before the Senate Government Affairs Committee on November 2, 1983, evidence was presented that General Dynamics sought to charge the Air Force $9,609 for a hexagonal wrench that could be purchased for $.12 and $7,417 for a 3″ steel pin that the Committee discovered they could get *free* in a Washington electronics store! The fact that such an outrageous attempt was even made is an indication of what General Dynamics and other government suppliers are obviously getting away with. Presumably if General Dynamics only sought to charge the government $10, $25 or $50 for these items (still outrageous) they probably could have got away with it! Can you imagine what defense contractors and other government suppliers *actually* get away with?

There is no doubt in my mind that given proper supervision, defense spending could probably be cut by 20% without any impairment in national defense.

The reason that taxpayers are so overcharged for national defense and other government services is that the President has to devote so much time to so many different government projects that he cannot give the necessary time and attention to the two areas for which he is specifically needed — national defense and foreign policy. In other words, the Federal government now sticks its nose into *so many areas* it cannot effectively do the job for which it is specifically charged under the Constitution and which *cannot* be done by local governments or private enterprise.

## Let's Have Real "Social Security"

To those who are fearful as to what this nation would be like without Social *in*Security, they need only consider what this nation was like, for example, in 1939. America had two World Fairs in 1939, one in San Francisco and the other in New York City. The people I recall seeing at the New York City fair were well dressed. There were roads with cars moving briskly along. America obviously made it to 1942 *without* Social *in*Security and I believe we were a healthier and mightier nation then than we are today. There is really nothing wrong with America that plowing under half of Washington, D. C. wouldn't cure. If there is anything to be said for Social *in*Security it is that the program can at least serve as a horrible example of the damage that politicians and bureaucrats can inflict on an unsuspecting public. So, to the extent that this program teaches the American people never to have faith in the economic promises and programs of the Federal government (nor allow it to do anything but run the Army, Navy and Air Force; maintain foreign embassies; and operate the courts and the F.B.I.), something good may yet come out of the forthcoming debacle.[13] If we terminate Social *in*Security and at least two other government programs[14] *at the same time,* the nation will quickly recover. In 5 years we will have a GNP double what it is today without unemployment or inflation. The American republic began with a tax rebellion and the nation is sorely in need of another one today!

## SUMMARIZING THE POINTS COVERED IN CHAPTER 10

1. America didn't need Social *in*Security before 1942 and it needs it even less now!

[13] As Tom Paine put it, "Government, even in its best state, is but a necessary evil; in its worst state, an intolerable one."

[14] Farm subsidies and minimum wage laws.

# Appendix A (Chapter 4 of The Biggest Con)

## Social Security: The World's Biggest Chain Letter

Leaving the government's currency flim-flam and fleecing by inflation, let's consider another multibillion-dollar fraud, Social Security.

Let me stress at the outset that there are *no monetary reserves* available to the Social Security System out of which future benefits can be paid. All past Social Security taxes collected by the government have been spent like regular taxes and never treated any differently. They were never deposited in any trust fund despite the many statements and assurances by the government that this was being done.

Government officials over the years have told the American public that Social Security is an "insurance program" employing sound principles of funding and financing. Nothing could be farther from the truth.

Let me offer some examples of how the government goes about "informing" the public about the structure and financial condition of the Social Security System, Figures 18, 19, and 20 are from Social Security publication No. SS1-50, and entitled "Your Medicare Handbook." Please note that *insurance* is used *six* times on the cover of the booklet (Figure 18), and on page 3 (Figure 19), it appears *eighteen* times. The usage of the

## Figure 18

# Your Medicare Handbook

HEALTH INSURANCE
UNDER
SOCIAL SECURITY

SSI-50
February 1974

HOSPITAL INSURANCE (PART A)
MEDICAL INSURANCE (PART B)

# Figure 19

## Like Medicare, your handbook has two parts. . .

### PART A

- The *first* section describes *hospital* insurance, often called *Part A* of Medicare. This is the part that helps pay for your care when you are in the hospital and for related health services, when you need them, after you leave the hospital.

### PART B

- The *second* section describes *medical* insurance, often called *Part B* of Medicare. This is the part that helps pay your doctor bills and bills for other medical services you need.

---

## Your Medicare health insurance card shows the protection you have

The people at the hospital, doctor's office, or wherever you get services, can tell from your health insurance card that you have both hospital and medical insurance and when each started. This is why you should always have your card with you when you receive services.

When a husband and wife both have Medicare, they receive separate cards and claim numbers.

If you ever lose your health insurance card, the people in your social security office will get you a new one.

# Figure 20

**Hospital Insurance—Part A of Medicare**

## You Get a Personal Record of Benefits Used

You don't have to bother about trying to keep track of how many "days" or "visits" you use in each benefit period. The notice you receive from the Social Security Administration after you have used any hospital insurance benefits will tell you how many benefit "days" and "visits" you have left in that benefit period. But, very few people who enter a hospital or extended care facility, or use home health services, need these services long enough to use all the benefits they have for a benefit period. So most people will never run out of "days" or "visits," because a new benefit period will almost always start with full benefits available again the next time they are needed.

***EXAMPLE:***

Mr. L was in the hospital for 2 weeks and then went home.

After Mr. L has been at home for 75 days, he returns to the hospital. When Mr. L is admitted this time, he is in a new benefit period. That means he is again eligible for up to 90 hospital days because more than 60 days have gone by since he was last in a hospital or other facility that mainly provides skilled nursing care. The benefit days Mr. L used the time before do not matter because he is in a new benefit period.

## How Hospital Insurance Benefits Are Financed

The hospital insurance program is financed by special contributions from employees and self-employed persons, with employers paying an equal amount. These contributions are collected along with regular social security contributions from the wages and self-employment income earned during a person's working years.

67 Until 1972, the contribution rate for the hospital insurance program is six-tenths of one percent of the first $7,800 of earnings. It will increase gradually until 1987 when it will reach the final rate of nine-tenths of one percent.

These contributions are put into the Hospital Insurance Trust Fund from which the program's benefits and administrative expenses are paid. Funds from general tax revenues are used to finance hospital insurance benefits for people who are covered under the program but are not entitled to monthly social security or railroad retirement benefits.

In addition, the law provides that the various dollar amounts for which the patient is responsible be reviewed annually. These dollar amounts include the first $40 of hospital charges in each benefit period and different per-day amounts after certain periods of benefit use in hospitals and extended care facilities. These are described on the following pages. The law also provides that if this annual review shows that hospital costs have changed significantly these amounts must be adjusted for the following year. However, no change in these amounts may be made before 1969.

word insurance is amazing when one considers that Social Security is not insurance. These numerous uses of the word, in my view, only emphasize the Social Security Administration's flagrant attempt to mislead the American public. Note the following statement in Figure 19. "Your Medicare Health Insurance Card shows the protection you have." "Insurance" serves no useful purpose in this sentence. The sentence should have read "Your Medicare card shows the protection you have".

Note the heading on the Medicare card—"Health Insurance". It would have been more accurate to simply title it "Medicare". Note the use of the phrase "name of beneficiary" on it. In insurance terminology, the beneficiary is a third party designated to receive a policy's benefits; it is never used to signify the *owner* or the *covered person*. *Covered person or name* would be a more accurate term. But the Social Security Administration chose to use insurance terminology even if incorrectly.

Note the first paragraph on that page "Part A": "The first section describes hospital insurance, often called Part A of Medicare." This could have read: "The first section describes the *hospital benefits* of Medicare, often called Part A". Part B should read: "The second section describes the *medical benefits* of Medicare, often called Part B". But, again "insurance" appears unnecessarily in both paragraphs.

In the section where the arrows are used in the lower left-hand portion, "insurance" is used *four* times. The card states "Is entitled to Hospital Insurance/Medical Insurance". It should read that the covered person is "entitled to Hospital Benefits and Medical Benefits". Although a person is normally entitled to *benefits,* he *pays* for *insurance*. Since insurance was already used on the Medicare card, good writing would dictate that the word "benefit" should be used, instead of "insurance". But "insurance" is used—and not just a few times, but 211 times in the 26 pages of this pamphlet!

## What Is Insurance?

Insurance has three general characteristics: (1) Insurance is a contract between an insuror and the insured whereby the insuror agrees to indemnify either the insured or a third-party beneficiary designated by the insured. The benefits itemized in the contract are enforceable in a court of law and are not subject to unilateral change. (2) Insurance attempts to relate the premiums and the costs of the insurance to the benefits and the risk involved—that is, the greater the risk, the higher the premium, or cost. Actuarial science is employed to achieve equity and financial stability. (3) Insurance companies are required to deposit premium income into a "reserve". This reserve is kept in cash accounts and the securities of *other* institutions. This reserve enables insurance companies to guarantee to pay the promised benefits. To determine the adequacy of its reserves, a company (a) assumes that it receives no new premiums and incurs no new liabilities after the evaluation date, and then (b) calculates whether the assets on hand, plus the interest they can earn in the future, are sufficient to meet future claims. If they are, then the company's insurance and pension liabilities are adequately funded. Let's apply this principle to a pension situation. Suppose a company had promised ten men aged 65 a $100 per-month pension for life. Mortality tables might show that the life expectancy of a man age 65 is 13 years. Obviously, some men in that group will not live that long, while others might outlive this period considerably. But for the purposes of establishing adequate reserves, we can rely on the known life expectancy for each man. So, starting at age 65, we can expect to pay each man $100 per month ($1,200 per year) or $15,600 over his life expectancy. Thus, we have committed ourselves to paying out nearly $156,000 to these ten men. Does this mean that, in order to discharge these future obligations, we must have $156,000 in our "reserve"? No, since while we are making these monthly payments, those assets in the reserve will be earning interest. If we assume that the assets in our reserve will earn 6 percent, we must have $108,140 in the reserve to pay the promised benefits. If we assume that our assets will only earn 4 percent, then we must begin with a larger reserve of $121,488.

Insurance company reserves are periodically examined by the insurance departments of the various states. If they're found to be deficient the company is suspended from doing business. It is actuarial reserves that differentiate insurance guarantees from other mere promises to pay. Applying the term insurance to a financial program which does not fund its future liabilities in the manner just described is to use the term erroneously, if not fraudulently.

## Is Social Security Insurance?

Let's examine Social Security in terms of the general characteristics of insurance.

1. Is there a legal, enforceable contract between the U.S. government and the citizen concerning Social Security benefits? No. Social Security benefits can be

changed or terminated at any time by Congress, and the government's right to confiscate individual Social Security benefits has been upheld in the courts (see *Fleming v. Nestor,* 80 S. Ct. 1367 [1960]).

2. There is, of course, little attempt to relate costs, risks, and benefits within the Social Security System. Wage earners pay the same OASDI taxes regardless of age, health, and degree of medical and disability risk involved. Recipients of Social Security benefits routinely have these benefits increased without ever having paid additional premiums.

3. How about reserves? The public, of course, is constantly reminded of the Social Security "trust fund". What constitutes this trust fund? Cash in a multitude of banks? Corporation stocks and bonds? Not at all. The U.S. Treasury reported that, as of June 30, 1973, the Federal Old Age Survivors Insurance Trust Fund, the Federal Disability Insurance Trust Fund, and the Federal Hospital Insurance Trust Fund collectively owned about $48 billion worth of government bonds, held in the "insurance trust funds" in order to help "defray" Social Security liabilities. This is the assumption that most people would make. However, this assumption is erroneous for government bonds are worthless in the hands of the government and are of no help to the government in meeting future Social Security liabilities. The only value that these bonds have is to help the government conceal the nature of these "insurance trust funds".

## Why All Government Bonds Held in So-Called Government "Trust Funds" Are Worthless

Most people regard a bond as an asset. If a government bond is an asset in the hands of a private citizen, then it is thought also to be an asset in the hands of the government. Quite the contrary. A bond is not an asset when held by the maker of the bond. For example suppose you gave someone and IOU (you, of course, recognize that a bond is nothing more than a formal IOU). That individual could treat your IOU as his asset. You, of course, could not write yourself an IOU and treat it as your asset. But this is what the government does when it passes off its bonds as "assets" of government "trust funds". The fact that the government routinely reports that their trust funds own approximately $48 billion of government bonds is indicative of not what the trust funds *own* but what the government *owes* them. Money that the government must pay to the trust funds to redeem these bonds can *only* be secured by taxing the citizens again for Social Security revenue for which they *had already been taxed and which had already been paid.*

Interestingly, even if the Social Security trust funds contained *legitimate* securities, they would only be a pittance compared to the actual amount that the trust funds should hold in order to pay the promised benefits. As shown in Chapter 3, in the "Statement of Liabilities and Other Financial Commitments of the United States Government as of June 30, 1973", the government's liability was nearly $2.118 billion (actually it was $3.3 trillion). Since these trust funds collectively owned only about $48 billion in government bonds, assets in the "insurance trust funds" would have had to be increased by at least 4,300 percent for them to have been actuarially sound. Since the Social Security System does not have actuarially sound trust funds, Social Security cannot be insurance.

Suffice it to say that not only would the insurance

commissioners of the various states shut down a company with an unfunded liability comparable to that of Social Security, but because of its reserve containing only notes of the company involved, they would also press charges against the company's officers for *fraud and grand larceny*. Insurance companies do not indiscriminately spend their premium income on projects and then leave their own IOUs (bonds) in the company till. If they did, they would be shut down and their officers carted off to jail.

All monies collected in the past through Social Security taxes have already been spent. This money was spent not only to meet past Social Security obligations, but to fight World War II, and the Korean and Vietnamese wars. It was used to bribe farmers not to grow food, finance Congressional junkets, support the U.N., and pay for landing on the moon. The bonds held by the Social Security trust funds are reminders of Social Security collections that have been spent on other projects.

Had the government taken past past Social Security taxes and invested them in American corporate bonds, the cash flow of these bonds plus their redemption value would help meet current Social Security obligations. This might have given the country a legitimate Social Security trust fund, but this was not done.

As further evidence of the U.S. government's deceiving of the American public about Social Security, we need only consider statements such as the following by Maurice Stans, a former Director of the Budget and a former Secretary of Commerce. In the following interview, reprinted from *U.S. News & World Report,* January 16, 1967, Stans was asked if he would do away with the Social Security trust fund, and just handle Social

Security as a direct obligation of the Treasury. To this he replied:

> I don't think it really makes any significant difference. There's now less money in the trust fund than is necessary to pay one year's benefits. We have long since abandoned the idea that President Roosevelt originally had when the Social Security fund was set up—the idea of keeping it on an actuarial basis so that the accumulated reserves would be equal at any date to the accrued retirement liabilities.
>
> We are now on a basis in which one year's collections from existing taxpayers are paid out in benefits to beneficiaries in the following year. So the trust fund has no particular significance as of now, except as an earmarking of taxes.

He was then asked:

> In what you said about the Social Security fund being adequate for less than one year's benefits, did you mean to imply that benefits are in danger in any way?

To which Stans answered:

> Oh, no—of course not. I merely imply that Social Security payments rest upon the general credit of the Government of the United States, upon its current taxing power, and not upon any accumulations in a trust fund to take care of you and me when we become eligible for benefits.
>
> 

Considering Mr. Stans' accounting background, he is qualified to render a judgment on the "significance" of the government's trust fund, which he does well;

however, he is hardly qualified to deliver an expert opinion concerning the *safety* of the payments that the System has promised to make. Stans should have responded to the second question by saying: "Yes, of course," since such an answer is implicit in his prior statement, which is why the question was asked. But, Social Security is sacrosanct, with few politicians daring to criticize it and expose it for what it really is.

Since the Social Security System does not operate on a legitimate reserve principle, as does insurance, then by what funding principle does it operate? The principle of the "chain letter"! Wage earners entering the bottom of the "chain" send their contributions, along with others moving up the "chain", to those workers who have made it to the top (those becoming eligible for benefits). Each new wave of entrants hopes, of course, that when it reaches the top, new waves of workers starting out at the bottom and those moving up will be forwarding benefits to them, thereby keeping the chain going. Is it conceivable that such an endless chain can really continue generation after generation? Look at what is happening. When Social Security was adopted, the maximum proposed tax was to be 3 percent withheld and 3 percent paid on a maximum salary of $3,000, *given a total proposed maximum tax of $180*. In 1975, with Social Security taxes at 5.85 percent, withheld and levied against payroll on a maximum salary of $14,100, the maximum tax reached $1,650.[1] In only 35 years, therefore, the maximum tax has soared over 800 percent. At this rate of increase (and Social Security taxes have been *increasing* at an *accelerating* rate)

[1] In 1984 it is 6.7% withholding, levied on a maximum of $37,800.

those who are now 25 could find the maximum tax at age 60 to be $13,000.

In the light of Stans' statements and in light of we have learned so far, let's examine Figure 20 (page 7 of *Your Medicare Handbook*). Please note its many errors and misleading statements. Notice the paragraphs beneath the caption "How Hospital Insurance Benefits are Financed" and in the first paragraph of that section the phrase, "with employers paying an equal amount". The Social Security Administration has always conveyed the impression to the American wage earner that he only pays half of the cost of Social Security and his employer pays the other. This is not true. The worker pays the *entire cost* of his Social Security. This becomes obvious when one understands the principle that a worker must produce enough to pay the entire cost of his employment, which includes direct and indirect wages. Also, money paid by employers in Social Security taxes reduces the amount that can be paid in wages. In any case, employers will treat Social Security taxes as simply another cost and pass it on in terms of higher prices. Therefore, the American worker must bear the entire cost of Social Security either in terms of lower wages or by paying higher prices.

Notice this line in the third paragraph: "These contributions are put into the Hospital Insurance Trust Fund from which the program's benefits and administrative expenses are paid". This statement is false because all Social Security receipts are immediately mixed with regular tax revenues where they all become available to meet various government expenditures.

Note in the second paragraph that Social Security *taxes* are *contributions*. *Contributions,* however, are voluntary payments. Social Security payments, as the IRS will speedily remind you, are *taxes* not *contributions*. This again is another Newspeak technique.

Please refer to Figures 21 and 22, the cover and page 8 of the IRS' 1975 "Employer's Tax Guide," respectively. Note how the government, when writing to employers concerning Social Security, consistently uses *taxes* when describing Social Security *payments*. *Taxes* appears 30 times in only two columns on page 8. Not once is *contribution* used. However, when the government produces pamphlets for public consumption (see Figures 18, 23, and 24 containing 26, 17, and 27 pages respectively), *taxes* is never mentioned, but *contributions* is used repeatedly. How should we account for this reverse terminology?

Please note Figure 23, a copy of page 7 from a pamphlet of the Department of Health, Education and Welfare, coded No. (SSA) 73-10033, and entitled "Social Security Information for Young Families." The final paragraph states:

> Financing of Social Security is examined each year by the Boards of Trustees of the trust funds. The latest report shows that the program is soundly financed both for the short-range and long-range future.

As was noted earlier[2], the Social Security System had unfunded liabilities of $2.118 trillion, which had increased from the previous year's liabilities by over $300 billion. This one year's increase in its unfunded liabilities was greater than the entire federal budget

[2] The government's unfunded liabilities were exhaustively examined in an earlier chapter of *The Biggest Con,* "The U.S. Public Debt And How The Government Cancelled It".

# Figure 21

Department of the Treasury
Internal Revenue Service

Third Class Bulk Rate
Postage and Fees Paid
Official Business
POSTMASTER: This matter must be forwarded and delivered without payment of postage due. If undeliverable after forwarding handle as specified in section 159.410.

## Circular E

# Employer's Tax Guide

### New Income Tax Withholding Rates and Tables

This revision of Circular E contains the revised rates and tables prescribed by the Department of the Treasury in accordance with the Tax Reduction Act of 1975 for withholding income tax from wages paid after April 30, 1975 and before January 1, 1976. The rates and tables take into account the new personal exemption credit, the increase in the standard deduction, and the new earned income credit.

A new Form W–4 (Revised April 1975), Employee's Withholding Allowance Certificate, is on pages 49 and 50. This new form with the revised table should be used by employees to determine the correct number of withholding allowances for itemized deductions that they are entitled to claim under the new law. Copies of Form W–4 are available at Internal Revenue District offices.

Please display the poster on page 51 of this circular on your bulletin board so that your employees will be aware of how the new law affects their tax withholding.

### Social Security Tax Base Increases

The maximum amount of wages subject to social security (FICA) taxes has been increased to $14,100 for wages paid in 1975.

### Magnetic Tape Reporting

Employers required to file wage and information documents are encouraged to do so on magnetic tape rather than on paper forms. See section 23, on page 10 for details.

Publication 15
(Rev. April 1975)

# Figure 22

## 18. Depositing Withheld Income Tax and Social Security (FICA) Taxes

**Note.** If any date shown falls on a Saturday, Sunday, or legal holiday, substitute the next regular workday.

Generally, you must deposit withheld income tax and social security taxes in an authorized commercial bank or a Federal Reserve bank. Include a Federal Tax Deposit Form 501 with each deposit. If you employ agricultural labor, you must include Federal Tax Deposit Form 511 with each deposit of the taxes on their wages.

The amount of taxes determines the frequency of deposits. Your liability for these taxes accrues when wages are paid, not when your payroll period ends. The following rules and examples show how often you must make deposits:

**(1) If at the end of a quarter, the total undeposited taxes are less than $200,** you are not required to make a deposit. You may either pay the taxes directly to the Internal Revenue Service along with your quarterly Form 941 or 941E, or make a deposit.

*Example:* At the end of the second quarter, the total undeposited taxes for the quarter are $170. Since this is less than $200, you may either pay the entire amount directly to the Internal Revenue Service with your quarterly Form 941 or 941E, or make a deposit.

**(2) If at the end of a quarter, the total undeposited taxes are $200 or more,** you must deposit the entire amount on or before the last day of the next month. If the undeposited amount is $2,000 or more, see rule 4 below.

*Example:* Your taxes for each month of the second quarter are $75. You must deposit $225 on or before July 31.

**(3) If at the end of any month (except the last month of a quarter), your cumulative undeposited taxes for the quarter are $200 or more and less than $2,000,** you must deposit the taxes within 15 days after the end of the month. (This does not apply if you made a deposit for a quarter-monthly period that occurred during the month under the $2,000 rule in 4 below.)

*Example A:* Your taxes for each of the first two months of the second quarter are $300. You must deposit $300 within 15 days after both April 30 and May 31.

*Example B:* Your taxes for each of the first two months of the second quarter are $150. You must deposit $300 within 15 days after May 31.

*Example C:* Your taxes are $500 for each month of the second quarter. You must deposit $500 within 15 days after both April 30 and May 31, and $500 on or before July 31.

**(4) If at the end of any quarter-monthly period, your cumulative undeposited taxes for the quarter are $2,000 or more,** you must deposit the taxes within 3 banking days after the end of the quarter-monthly period. (Quarter-monthly periods end on the 7th, 15th, 22d, and last day of any month.) To determine banking days, exclude any local banking holidays observed by authorized commercial banks as well as Saturdays, Sundays, and legal holidays. You will meet the deposit requirements if: (a) you deposit at least 90 percent of the actual tax liability for the deposit period, and (b) if the quarter-monthly period occurs in a month other than the third month of a quarter, you deposit any underpayment with your first deposit that is required to be made after the 15th day of the following month. Any underpayment of $200 or more for a quarter-monthly period that occurs during the third month of the quarter must be deposited on or before the last day of the month.

*Example A:* During April your taxes for each quarter-monthly period are $3,000. You must deposit $3,000 within 3 banking days after April 7, 15, 22, and 30.

*Example B:* During the second quarter your taxes for each quarter-monthly period are $700. You must deposit $2,100 within 3 banking days after April 22, May 15, June 7, and June 30.

# Figure 22 (continued)

**Summary of Deposit Rules for Withheld Income Tax and Social Security Taxes**

| Deposit rule | Deposit due |
|---|---|
| 1. If at the end of a quarter the total undeposited taxes are less than $200: | No deposit required. Pay balance directly to the Internal Revenue Service with your quarterly return, or make a deposit if you prefer. |
| 2. If at the end of a quarter the total undeposited taxes are $200 or more: | On or before last day of next month. If $2,000 or more, see rule 4. |
| 3. If at the end of any month (except the last month of a quarter), cumulative undeposited taxes for the quarter are $200 or more, but less than $2,000: | Within 15 days after end of month. (For the first 2 months of the quarter no deposit is required if you previously made a deposit for a quarter-monthly period that occurred during the month under the $2,000 rule in item 4, below.) |
| 4. If at the end of any quarter-monthly period, cumulative undeposited taxes for the quarter are $2,000 or more: | Within 3 banking days after the quarter-monthly period ends. |

## 19. Using Government Depositories

**How to Deposit Taxes.**—Fill in a pre-inscribed Federal Tax Deposit Form 501 or Form 508, depending on the type of tax you are depositing, according to instructions.

Send each Federal tax deposit form and a single payment covering the taxes to be deposited to any commercial bank qualified as a depository for Federal taxes, or to a Federal Reserve bank. Make checks or money orders payable to the bank where you make your tax deposit. Contact your local bank or Federal Reserve bank for the names of authorized commercial bank depositories.

The timeliness of deposits is determined by the date the bank receives them. A deposit received by the bank after the due date will be considered timely if you establish that you mailed it 2 or more days before the due date.

**How to Obtain Federal Tax Deposit Forms.**—The Service will automatically send you pre-inscribed Federal tax deposit forms after you apply for an identification number. If you need additional forms, order them from the Internal Revenue Service Center where you file. Be sure to show your name, employer identification number, address, periods for which the forms are needed, and type of tax. Request forms early.

If your branch offices make tax deposits, obtain a supply of Federal tax deposit forms and distribute them to the branches so they can make deposits when due.

Do not use another employer's pre-inscribed forms. If you have not received Federal tax deposit forms by a deposit due date, mail your payment to the Internal Revenue Service Center where you file your return. Make it payable to the Internal Revenue Service and show on it your name, identification number, address, kind of tax, and period covered.

**Deposit Record.**—Before making a deposit, enter the payment amount on the form and stub, and record the check or money order number and date. Keep the stub for your records. The Service will not return the deposit portion of this form to you, but will use it to credit your tax account by means of your employer identification number.

**How to Claim Credit for Overpayments.**—If you deposited more than the correct amount of taxes for a quarter, you may elect to have the overpayment refunded, or applied as a credit to your next return. Show the appropriate for that year, while the total unfunded liabilities of the Social Security System was nearly five times greater (even using the government's own understated figures) than the entire reported national debt! This, therefore, hardly qualifies as a program that is "soundly financed both for the short-range and the long-range future." *Social Security obligations are not "financed" at all, as the pamphlet unabashedly claims.*

Figure 24 is a reproduction of pages 22 and 23 of HEW pamphlet 75-10035 issued November 1974 and entitled "Your Social Security." These two pages contain no less than *thirty-one* misstatements of fact and/or misleading inferences regarding Social Security.

The many misstatements in the three Social Security pamphlets cited are good examples of how the government and the Social Security Administration have deliberately misled the American public regarding Social Security's solvency and character.

To that extent, these pamphlets are blatant violations of Section 1001, Title 18, of the U.S. criminal code, a section I cited earlier. The statement in pamphlet 73-10033 that "the latest report shows the program [Social Security] is soundly financed both for the short-range and long-range future" is so blantantly false, given the Treasury Department's report of June 30, 1973, that those who approved this pamphlet should receive diciplinary action immediately. And, of course, both "Your Medicare Handbook" and "Your Social Security" are fraught with statements that are false, fictitious, and fraudulent.

## What Are "Social Forms of Insurance"?

When government actuaries and bureaucrats find themselves trapped by intelligent questions about So-

# Figure 23

**Kinds of work covered**
Almost every kind of employment and self-employment is covered by social security. Some occupations and some kinds of earnings, however, are affected by special provisions of the law.

If the kind of work you do is listed below and you aren't sure if you are earning protection under social security, you may want to ask someone at your social security office for information on these special provisions:

▼
Family employment—work done by a child under 21 for a parent, work done by a spouse, or work done by a parent in the home of a child;

▼
Work in or about the private home of your employer;

▼
Student employment at a school or college;

▼
Farm work; or

▼
Employment in a job where you get cash tips.

**Financing social security**
Social security retirement, survivors, and disability benefits and hospital insurance benefits are paid for by contributions based on covered earnings.

If you are employed, the contributions are deducted from your salary, and your employer pays an equal amount; if you are self-employed, you contribute at a little over ⅔ the combined employee-employer rate for retirement, survivors, and disability insurance. The hospital insurance contribution rate is the same for employers, employees, and self-employed persons.

The maximum amount of yearly earnings that can count for social security and on which you pay social security contributions is $13,200 for 1974. The maximum will increase automatically in later years to keep pace with increases in average earnings.

The maximum in past years was: $3,000 a year for 1937-50; $3,600 for 1951-54; $4,200 for 1955-58; $4,800 for 1959-65; $6,600 for 1966-67; $7,800 for 1968-71; $9,000 for 1972; and $10,800 for 1973.

People now making social security contributions can be sure that funds will be available to pay their benefits when they become eligible. The schedule of contribution rates now in the law will provide income sufficient to pay all benefits under present law as well as administrative costs of the program now and into the future. Financing of social security is examined each year by the Boards of Trustees of the trust funds. The latest report shows that the program is soundly financed both for the short-range and long-range future.

# Figure 24

## Financing

**The basic idea**
The basic idea of social security is a simple one: During working years employees, their employers, and self-employed people pay social security contributions into special trust funds. When earnings stop or are reduced because the worker retires, becomes disabled, or dies, monthly cash benefits are paid to replace part of the earnings the family has lost.

Part of the contributions made go into a separate hospital insurance trust fund so workers and their dependents will have help in paying their hospital bills when they become eligible for Medicare. The medical insurance part of Medicare is financed by premiums paid by the people who have enrolled for this protection and amounts contributed by the Federal Government.

**Contribution rates**
If you're employed, you and your employer each pay an equal share of social security contributions. If you're self-employed, you pay contributions for retirement, survivors, and disability insurance at a somewhat lower rate than the combined rate for an employee and his employer. The hospital insurance contribution rate is the same for the employer, the employee, and the self-employed person.

As long as you have earnings that are covered by the law, you continue to pay contributions egardless of your age and even if you are receiving social security benefits.

Through 1977 employees and employers each pay 5.85 percent on the employee's wages. The total rate for self-employed people is 7.90 percent. The rates include .90 percent for hospital insurance under Medicare. The maximum amount of earnings that can count for social security purposes and on which you pay social security contributions is $14,100 in 1975.

Future rate increases are scheduled. In 1978 the employee and employer will each pay 6.05 percent. The rate for each will go to 6.30 percent in 1981 and 6.45 percent in 1986. The self-employed rate goes to 8.10 percent in 1978; to 8.35 percent in 1981; and to 8.50 percent in 1986. The hospital insurance part of the rate will be 1.10 percent in 1978; 1.35 percent in 1981; and 1.50 percent in 1986.

Funds not required for current benefit payments and expenses are invested in interest-bearing U.S. Government securities.

The Government's share of the cost for supplementary medical insurance and certain other social security costs come from general revenues of the U.S. Treasury, not from social security contributions.

**How contributions are paid**
If you're employed, your contribution is deducted from your wages each payday. Your employer matches your payment and sends the combined amount to the Internal Revenue Service.

If you're self-employed and your net earnings are $400 or more in a year, you must report your earnings and pay your self-employment contribution each year when you file your individual income tax return. This is true even if you owe no income tax.

Your wages and self-employment income are entered on your social security record throughout your working years. This record of your earnings will be used to determine cial Security's deficiencies, they try to evade the fact that Social Security is a Ponzi-like scheme by replying, "but Social Security is a social form of insurance and, as such, it is not susceptible to the same type of measurement and actuarial standards as private forms of insurance". Such assertions are absurd. Either something is insurance or it isn't.

What are "social forms of insurance," if they are not insurance? They are simply forms of "socialism" (see Chapter 6,[3] for discussion on socialism). "Social forms of insurance" is socialism sold to the public as an adjunct of the free-enterprise system, since its proponents use capitalistic terms, such as *insurance, reserves, funding,* and *premiums,* which are non-existant in a socialistic lexicon. "Social forms of insurance" is actually a cryptosocialistic term; it promotes socialism under the guise and within the framework of the free-enterprise system.

## How Social Security Lowers America's Standard of Living

One of the tragedies of Social Security is that it has helped (and helps) to lower the American standard of living. One reason for this is that Social Security has spawned a large, nonproductive class of bureaucrats whose sole function is to service this vast system, while at the same time imposing uneconomic and unnecessary collection and record-keeping burdens on American industry.

I often wonder how many American businesses that are now forced to close their doors (thus creating unemployment and social *insecurity*) would remain

[3] Refers to Chapter 6 of *The Biggest Con.*

open if only they had as working capital the money they had paid into Social Security during the last five years.

Another tragedy in connection with Social Security is that the government has convinced vast segments of the public that the System will be able to provide them with significant income during their later years. This, of course, will not be possible. An objective analysis of the assets and liabilities of the System, together with the growth rate of these liabilities, plus the declining growth rate and the declining productive base of the economy (in large measure due to the economy being saddled with such inane government programs and burdensome taxes) will point toward the System's collapse. The only question is when? Therefore, many will be without the income they had expected. Had Social Security "contributions" not been compulsory, the money could have been invested elsewhere in the private sector. Substantial capital, in this way, would have been channeled into the private sector, increasing the country's industrial base, and creating more jobs and goods — in sum, generating real growth. Instead, this capital was channeled to Washington where it was largely dissipated by politicians and bureaucrats.

Perhaps the greatest tragedy of the Social Security System is that each month over 30 million recipients[4] of Social Security are told that if they earn more than a stated sum, they will lose part if not all of their benefits. How many millions of these recipients might, in fact, be capable and willing to work if only they were not discouraged and penalized from doing so by government? A nation's standard of living is determined by the total economic output of its citizens. If fewer people work,

[4] To recipients under 16, such prohibitions are, I grant, immaterial.

then the lower the nation's productivity and its standard of living become. Thus, since Social Security actually encourages, even compels, nonproductivity by a vast segment of the population, it is forcing a substantially lower standard of living on the entire nation.

# *Appendix B (Pages 302-304, The Biggest Con)*

## Who Is Liable for Political Irresponsibility?

In the final analysis it boils down to this: Is the nation's current generation of producers (especially those in their twenties), who are themselves struggling with families and careers, liable for the unrealistic economic promises of past generations of irresponsible politicans? Did politicians long-gone have the right to indenture unborn generations of Americans to the service of other Americans, simply to make good on their irresponsible campaign promises?

The answer is obvious—No! And the bitter price that must now be paid for this fiscal folly must be borne by those Americans who bought the promises—not the nation's young men and women who had nothing whatever to do with it. Americans now reaching 65 were not (at age 20) saddled with the burden of having to support a large retired, disabled, and dependent population—and today's twenty-year-old Americans are entitled to the same consideration. So, where do we go from here?

## Deflating the Transfer Payments Bubble

Once the nation realizes that Social Security is defunct, it can begin to handle the consequences more intelligently. The first thing that has to be done is to institute a realistic "needs" test for future Social Security payments. There are some citizens who might have no other source of income and who would be destitute without Social Security payments, while obviously there are others, (retired millionaires, for instance) who also receive Social Security, but who could survive without it. Between these two extremes there will be degrees of need, which must be evaluated in determining the levels of Social Security payments, taking into consideration age, financial circumstances, health, and one's employment potential.

The fact that one paid Social Security taxes in the past cannot now determine the receipt of such payments in the future. If it makes citizens feel any better, they should simply regard their past Social Security taxes as merely an indication of a prior higher ordinary tax rate (which is precisely what it was), while all those who are currently receiving "benefits" should regard such "benefits" as welfare checks. Thus, a taxpayer who thought he was paying a Social Security tax of 5 percent while being in a 25 percent tax bracket, was really in a 30 percent bracket and paying these taxes, so that the U.S. government could make welfare payments to many citizens who were far wealthier than the taxpayer.

Since Social Security is "financed" on the same basis as welfare, welfare standards obviously must apply. Future Social Security "benefits" will have to be based on need. The country has no other alternative.

It is not necessary at this time for me to attempt to outline in detail a program for reforming Social Security. I will, however, suggest a brief outline for such a program:

1. A needs test, as I have suggested, will have to be immediately instituted.

2. The Social Security tax itself would be abolished and regular tax rates adjusted accordingly.

3. No Social Security recipient should be penalized because of the receipt of earned income.

4. A sliding scale of reduced future benefits should be projected over the next ten years for those otherwise eligible for current benefits. This would enable future Social Security claimants to plan their retirement more realistically. Obviously, the farther an individual is from 65, the more time he has to adjust to the phasing out of the program.

5. A target date must be established for the official termination of the entire program—say, December 31, 1987. This would allow for gradual phasing out, enabling and encouraging individuals to seek more dependable sources of support for their later years than mere political promises.

A needs test would bar Social Security "benefits" to many now receiving them. However, before such individuals despair over losing their Social Security "benefits," they should recognize that, actually, they were not receiving any "benefits" in the first place. For example, suppose a retired widow or widower with approximately $50,000 in cash assets, such as CDs, bonds, and savings accounts, received the maximum Social Security monthly benefit of approximately $300 a month, or $3,600 a year. During 1974, the inflationary activities of the government (both in increasing the money supply and interfering with the production of goods) were responsible for at least an 18 percent rate of inflation (official figures of 12.2 percent notwithstanding). This rate of inflation would have caused a loss in this individual's liquid savings of $9,000. Therefore, the inflation generated by the government so that it could make unrealistic Social Security payments would have *cost* this individual $5,400. Furthermore, if the above individual had income from a private pension or annuity of $400 monthly, or $4,800 annually, the government, through its inflationary activities, would have reduced the value of these annuity payments by an *additional* $864. It should be further recognized that stock values plummeted in 1974 largely because of government economic and monetary policies and the high taxes paid by corporations. So in addition to the above dollar assets, if the individual started 1974 with stock worth $50,000, he would have suffered stock losses (conservatively estimated) of at least 15 percent of $7,500, as a result of unstable market conditions caused by government economic and fiscal policy. In addition, inflationary losses applied to its year-end value of another 18 percent would have yielded additional losses of $7,650. So this individual would have suffered inflationary tax losses of $16,650 and additional government-related equity losses of $7,500 for a total government-related loss of $25,014 sustained by him in order to receive $3,900 from the government. Obviously, such individuals cannot afford such government "benefits"—they are *too expensive*. It is apparent that this person, like others who apply these same financial adjustments to their own asset portfolios, would discover that he is getting nothing from government in the way of real purchasing power through Social Security. So by eliminating Social Security payments, we eliminate *nothing,* while if we do not quickly eliminate such payments in an orderly fashion, they will be eliminated *anyway* (in my judgment, in from three to five years), in an atmosphere of financial and social chaos with recipients losing a good deal more than merely paper checks.

So, by simultaneously scaling sown Social Security and cutting out government and government waste, we will be restoring to the nation's retired citizens a good deal that is now being taken from them.

Much of the same reasoning will, of course, apply to persons receiving any "income payments" from the government. Many now receiving such payments are losing far more because of the shrinkage in the purchasing power of their other assets than they are gaining by way of their government "pensions." So, even if they were to lose a portion or all of these promised government "benefits," they would be gaining far more than they would be losing.

In addition, and I feel it bears repeating, those who feel that they are "entitled" to government pensions must keep in mind that if all those who feel similarly "entitled" insist on pressing their claims, they will succeed in forcing the financial collapse of U.S. Government, Inc., and will thereby create (for themselves and the rest of the economy) a situation where they will not only end up losing their pensions anyway, but in the process also lose their accumulated savings, the value of their private pensions, the value of their bonds, and a substantial portion of the value of their common stock.

# *Appendix C*

**FIGURE 50**

Mr. Fred Hardnose
ABC COMPANY
Main Street
Fairfax, Connecticut 00001

Dear Mr. Hardnose:

Attached please find my affidavit attesting to the fact that I have no "income" subject to tax pursuant to Section 3101 of the Internal Revenue Code (commonly referred to as "social security" tax).

I, therefore, instruct you to immediately stop withholding such taxes from my wages as of the date of this letter.

Sincerely,

Ima Freeman

Attached: Affidavit

| IMA FREEMAN | : | SUPERIOR COURT |
|---|---|---|
| VS. | : | JUDICIAL DIST. |
| FRED HARDNOSE | : | STATE OF CONN. |
| | : | DATE: Feb. 1, 1984 |

## COMPLAINT

1. The plaintiff is a resident of the town of Fairfax within the county of Plymouth and is an employee of the defendant Fred hardnose within said town.

2. The defendant is a manufacturer of buttons and employs the plaintiff and others.

3. On or about __________ , 1983, the plaintiff delivered to the defendant the letter and supporting affidavit (attached hereto as Exhibits A and B respectively) directing the defendant to immediately stop withholding any sums of money from his/her pay for income taxes pursuant to 26 U.S.C. Section 3101 (commonly called "social security") in that the plaintiff declared he/she has no income subject to said tax. *(Attach copy of letter marked "Exhibit A" and copy of Affidavit marked "Exhibit B".)*

4. Yet despite the plaintiff's request and sworn declaration that he/she has no income subject to such tax nor has plaintiff been made liable for such tax pursuant to 26 U.S.C. Sections 6201, 6303 and 6203, the defendant has continued to withhold a portion of the plaintiff's wages from him/her purportedly on behalf of such a tax.

5. There is no provision of the U.S. Internal Revenue Code which establishes a "liability" or any "require-

ment" that the plaintiff pay such tax nor is the word "income", as used in 26 U.S.C. Section 3101, defined (see *U.S. vs. Ballard,* 535 F2d 400, page 404).

6. The defendant Fred Hardnose, by his actions, as aforesaid, has deprived the plaintiff of his property without due process of law and without compensation in violation of the Fifth Amendment to the United States Constitution and of the Connecticut Constitution, Article 1, Section 7 (freedom from unreasonable seizures) and Article 1, Section 11 (freedom from taking of private property without just compensation).

7. The defendant has withheld the sum of $ ________ as of this date and by information and belief intends to continue to so withhold the money earned by the plaintiff.

WHEREFORE THE PLAINTIFF CLAIMS:

1. Money damages.

2. An Order requiring the defendant to return to plaintiff funds withheld from his/her wages from the date of the receipt of notification from the plaintiff that he should stop withholding funds from plaintiff's wages together with interest thereon.

3. An Order requiring the defendant to refrain from withholding funds from plaintiff's wages pursuant to 26 U.S.C. Section 3101 until such time as plaintiff shall have notified him of a change in plaintiff's income status or until such time as he shall be notified by the

Secretary of the Treasury that the plaintiff has been duly "assessed" and "made liable" for Section 3101 "income taxes" pursuant to Sections 6201, 6203 and 6303 of the Internal Revenue Code.

Hereof fail not but due service and return make.

Dated at Fairfax, Connecticut this ____ day of ______, 198____.

THE PLAINTIFF

______________________________

Pro Se

Note: This is an example of a State Court complaint. It is to be used *only* as a sample form. The form should be adapted to meet your particular needs and the rules of your State Court. Seek advice from the clerk's office of your State Court. Information in the complaint that is underlined should be replaced with your own personal information before submission.

# Appendix D

The Federal government couldn't have pulled off the Social Security caper without getting a lot of help from "experts" in the private sector. I offer two cases in point:

## Paul Samuelson

Probably no one has done more to scramble the brains of American youth on the subject of economics than MIT's Professor Paul A. Samuelson.[1] Apart from his being a special economics advisor to Presidents Kennedy and Johnson and winning the Nobel Prize for Economics in 1970, he authored *Economics: An Introductory Analysis,* which has probably been used by more college students than any other economics text. So, if you've ever discussed economics with one of your college-trained sons or daughters — and if they didn't seem to make any sense whatsoever — chances are they used Samuelson's text.

For example, in his third edition (published in 1958) he states that in comparison to Social Security, "A private insurance company would have to charge tens of thousands of dollars for such generous annuities and privileges . . .". (See *The Biggest Con,* page 181.) Samuelson apparently believes that tens of thousands of dollars of insurance benefits and privileges can be

[1] See *The Biggest Con,* pages 233-241

produced by the Federal government out of thin air at no cost to anyone! That observation was followed by this gem: "It is one of the great advantages of a pay-as-you-go Social Security system that it rests on the general tax capacity of the nation; if hyperinflation wiped out all private insurance and savings, Social Security could, nonetheless, start all over again, none the poorer." Start all over with what? The economy would be in a shambles! Samuelson obviously belongs to the Alice-in-Wonderland School of Economics! Even with an economic calamity in which all private savings are wiped out, Social Security recipients have nothing to worry about! If the above situation did, indeed, happen, all economic activity would come to a screeching halt.[2]

But, even in this situation, Samuelson believes that the government's "tax capacity" (i.e. the nation's economic health) has not changed and that Social Security's recipients are, therefore, "none the poorer". Stop shaking your head in disbelief, the man *really did* win a Noble Prize in Economics!

As proof that Samuelson did not seem to learn much as the years passed, I offer this quote from his February 13, 1967 column in *Newsweek* magazine:

> "The beauty about social insurance is that it is actuarially *unsound.* Everyone who reaches retirement age is given *benefit privileges* that *far exceed anything he has paid in.* And exceed his payments by more than ten times as much (or five times, counting in employer payments). How is this possible? It stems from the fact that the national product is growing at a compound interest and can be expected to do so for as far ahead as the eye can see. Always there are more youths than folks in a growing population. More important, with

[2] In this situation, transportation would also come to a halt — since how could anyone pay their bills? Food and other necessities would not be available in our stores. One can only speculate on the rioting and pillaging that would take place as people scrambled to get the necessities of life.

> real incomes growing at some 3 percent per year, the taxable base upon which benefits rest in any period are much greater than the taxes paid historically by the generation now retired." (emphasis added)

So apparently Samuelson is overjoyed that Social Security is "actuarially unsound" and believes that without anyone working harder and longer (and without any apparent increase in capital) we all are going to have *more*! He bases his amazing conclusion on his belief that the ". . . national product is growing. . ." (and will continue to *magically* grow) ". . .at compound interest and can be expected to do so for as far ahead as the eye can see".

Well, thanks to economic policies shaped by such ludicrous beliefs, real incomes in America have dropped each year for the past 10 years, while the nation's real economic output (in terms of goods) is falling like a lead balloon. This is why the majority of Americans today cannot afford to buy homes; are driving much smaller cars than did their parents and grandparents; and are forced to use a lot less energy. Which, in turn, increasingly compels more wives to work (unlike American mothers and grandmothers in the past) just to keep the family's economic nose above water.

## Sylvia Porter

Sylvia Porter's brand of "economics" is spread to millions of Americans via her popular column that appears in newspapers throughout the nation. In addition, she has authored best-selling books on income taxes and investments. While I am not fortunate enough to see Ms. Porter's column on a regular basis, I do get to read it from time to time and did see the four-part series on Social Security she did in February, 1976. These excerpts are from the fourth part of that series which appeared on February 5th.

Ms. Porter concedes that "There are cruel inequities in the Social Security law. . .", such as "provisions that discriminate against women and the dependents of women workers" and provisions "that penalize older people who work" (the system presumably should then be *liberalized* to include such individuals). And, further, that there are, indeed, "financing problems which Congress must tackle and solve to keep this basic program up-to-date and effective". She, nevertheless, felt that Social Security was the "target" of unfair criticism while her criticisms,on the other hand, she believed were ". . . fair, objective criticisms, neither inviting panic nor insisting that all is in perfect order".

She proceeded to inveigh against those who suggest that Social Security be made voluntary which, she pointed out, "would be the death of our Social Security System, the abandonment of the program's fundamental purpose — to a floor of protection for all our citizens and prevent poverty before it occurs". Porter then told her readers how lucky they were to have Social Security. "Even with the best of intentions," they were told, "millions of you simply would not set aside money regularly — particularly if you are low income workers or have a growing family. When you reached your older years, became disabled or died, you or your survivors would be forced onto the welfare roles, with your payments financed out of general Federal revenues and state and local taxes. The cost to taxpayers would still be there, but the worker would not have contributed".

Here, of course, the implication is that the government would "set aside money" for participants in Social Security since individuals ("even with the best intentions") would not do so for themselves. Representations like this by presumed "experts," such as Ms. Porter, help create the illusion in the minds of the public that the government is actually "saving" their money. These representations are, of course, sheer nonsense! Another misconception that Ms. Porter helped create is that without Social Security individuals would be forced onto the welfare roles. This line of thinking entirely overlooks the fact that individuals not compelled to pay Social Security taxes would have had far more money to purchase far better (and more secure) life insurance, disability protection and retirement plans than could be provided by government.[3] For a time the government was able to provide *unrealistic* benefits in the *short run* — which means that many Americans will end up with *nothing* in the *long run*!

Her concern that without Social Security "you and your survivors would be forced onto the welfare roles, with your payments financed out of general revenues", reveals that Ms. Porter does not understand that Social Security benefits have *always* come from "general revenues". All tax collections go into a common pot and are used by the government to pay *all* of its bills. Does Porter believe that Social Security payments are paid out of some special cash reserve which the government keeps in a shoe box? Or, perhaps payments are paid by selling off government assets? She obviously doesn't understand that, in reality, recipients of Social Security are, indeed, paid on exactly the same financial basis as those on "the welfare roles".

Social Security recipients receive money and benefits taken from current taxpayers (many of whom have trouble paying their own bills) on exactly the same basis as current workers are taxed to pay benefits to those on "the welfare roles". True, those receiving

[3] Overlooking completely the additional revenues and lower costs that would result from all this capital flowing into the private sector instead of being totally dissipated by government through taxation.

Social Security benefits might have, themselves, paid Social Security taxes in the past; but many on welfare also might have paid taxes in the past. Presumably then, welfare recipients are "entitled" to welfare benefits for the same reason that those who pay Social Security taxes are "entitled" to Social Security benefits.

Ms. Porter then pointed out that millions of people might "faithfully invest what you would have paid in Social Security taxes. . .you would not find a private insurance policy providing the comprehensive package of protection you now get from Social Security: retirement insurance, disability insurance, life insurance, health insurance for your older years. Even if you were able to put such a package together, it would cost far more than what you pay in Social Security taxes". Such an observation was, of course, more nonsense and demonstrated that she simply does not understand the nature of either insurance or Social Security — two subjects on which she is *supposed to be* an "expert."

She further said that even if people were "astute — or lucky — enough to create an investment portfolio that would give you the same return as Social Security, most of you would end up short of your goal or wiped out." I must ask Ms. Porter if Social Security *really* creates "an investment portfolio"? If not, why then did she make such a misleading comparison? As far as being wiped out is concerned, I leave it to the reader to decide which "investment portfolio" they would prefer — the one recommended by Ms. Porter or any average mutual fund?

The implications in both Professor Samuelson's and Ms. Porter's statements are variations on the same theme — the public will get "investment and insurance" bargains from the Federal government. So, with the government deliberately misstating the facts with respect to Social Security on one hand, and with the (mis)information the public got (and continues to get) from private sector "experts" on the other, the Federal government was able to pull off the largest Ponzi scheme the world has ever seen.

# *Legal Cases Cited*

*Bente vs. Bugbee* 103 NJL 608
*Brushaber vs. Pacific RR* 240 U.S. 1
*Cairo Fulton RR vs. Hecht* 95 U.S. 170
*Carter vs. Carter Coal Co.* 298 U.S. 238
*Davis vs. Boston I.M.R. Co.* 89 F2d 368
*Davis vs. Edison Electric Illuminating Co. of Boston et al* 89 F2d 393
*Flint vs. Stone Tracy Co.* 220 U.S. 107
*Gleason vs. McKay* 134 Mass 419
*Helvering vs. Davis* 301 U.S.C. 619
*Marbury vs. Madison* 1 CR. 137
*McCulloch vs. Maryland* 4 Wheat. 316 (1819)
*Miller vs. Illinois C.R. Co.* 146 Miss 422
*O'Keefe vs. Somerville* 190 Mass 110
*Patton vs. Brady* 184 U.S. 608
*Pollack vs. Farmer's Loan & Trust Co.* 158 U.S. 429
*Steward Machine Co. vs. Davis* 301 U.S. 548
*U.S. vs. Ballard* 535 F2d 400

# *Reading List*

All books available through Freedom Books, PO Box 5303, Hamden, Connecticut 06518. Prices are denoted by ∅ which refers to Federal Reserve units — fiat currency now fraudulently circulating as U.S. dollars, and include postage and handling. Please allow 4-6 weeks for delivery.

## *BOOKS AND MATERIALS BY IRWIN SCHIFF*

***The Schiff Report*** ........................ *∅75.00/year*

An indispensible publication for those who want detailed instructions on how to protect yourself from the IRS. Provides information nowhere else available including documents, sample legal instruments and procedures to use against the IRS. Many subscribers report that each issue is worth the price of the subscription. Also contains Irwin Schiff's economic and political comentary. 8 issues per calendar year. Newsletter format.

## *BOOKS:*

*How Anyone Can Stop Paying Income Taxes* ....... *∅12.00*

Published in 1982, this unbelievable book has become the nation's best-selling hard cover book on Federal income taxes. Now in its fifth printing the book has sold over 185,000 copies and neither the IRS nor any tax attorney has ever attempted to refute one word of it. Read this book and discover for yourself the hoax of the Federal income tax and never again pay a dime in "income" taxes, file an "income" tax return or be audited. This book will set you free!!

*The Biggest Con: How The Government is Fleecing You* .................................... *∅9.00*

Provides irrefutable evidence of the criminal and destructive nature of the Federal government. "The single most important book on the status of this nation I have ever read," said Howard Ruff, editor of *The Ruff Times*. Soft cover.

*The Kingdom of Moltz* .............................. *∅3.00*

A delightful tale of our monetary system written so that even a child of ten can understand it. "I laughed so hard I cried. Schiff's book is the greatest thing since sliced bread," commented Dr. Camille Castorina, economics professor at St. John's University. Paperback.

*The Tax Rebel's Guide to the Constitution and Declaration of Independence* .......................... *∅2.50*

The guide is color coded to call attention to particular clauses which should be of special interest to those

Americans interested in preserving their constitutional rights. Paperback.

*Why No One Can Have Taxable Income*

*Soon to be published*

This book will explain why no individual or corporation can have income that is subject to a compulsory income tax under the Internal Revenue Code. This book will enable you to challenge any attempt by the IRS to assess or collect any income taxes (current or back) allegedly owed by you.

## *AUDIO-VISUAL MATERIALS:*

Over the last seven years thousands of Americans have been enlightened and entertained by Irwin Schiff's famous Untax Seminars. His latest seminar lecture (directly related to the material in *How Anyone Can Stop Paying Income Taxes)* has now been recorded on audio and video tape cassettes. Taped before a live audience, you can see and hear for yourself how you can drop out and join the thousands of others who have done the same. Please specify:

*Three hour video tape*
*(VHS - LP) .......................Ø65.00*
*Three hour video tape*
*(Beta Max - Betax 2) ..............Ø65.00*

*Two Audio Tapes (C-90) .............Ø15.00*

New, 50-minute television show that was produced in Hollywood is now available. Suitable for airing on local/cable TV it is also available on standard VHS or BETA MAX cassettes. An excellent educational tool, this show is also entertaining and will quickly convince you that you are not required to file Federal income taxes. Please specify:

*50-Minute TV Special (VHS) .........∅99.00*
*50-Minute TV Special (Beta Max) .....∅99.00*

*For information and pricing on ¼" or ½" tape for TV airing please contact FREEDOM BOOKS, (203) 281-1470.*

## *ALSO RECOMMENDED*

*The Complete Internal Revenue Code ..............∅18.00*

In order to effectively fight the IRS, each citizen should have a copy of the Internal Revenue Code since the IRS will misleadingly state the law and attempt to confuse you regarding IRS regulations (which are not binding when they conflict with the law — as many of them do).

# The Schiff Report

*A journal committed to the restoration of limited, constitutional government, the free enterprise system, and honest money; and therefore dedicated to the abolishment of the income tax and the Federal Reserve.*

*The Schiff Report* provides up-to-date information on how to protect yourself from the IRS in specific situations:

- How to prevent the IRS from getting bank records.
- How to handle employers who may be intimidated by the IRS into not honoring your W-4.
- How to apply for refunds.
- How to amend prior returns.
- How to handle third party IRS summonses.
- News of the tax rebellion.
- Court wins throughout the country.
- Economic and political commentary.
- Techniques and strategies for fighting the IRS.

Annual subscription price (8 issues/year) is $75.00. Subscriptions will begin with Volume 2, Number 1 unless otherwise requested.